IS
THIS
ANYTHING?

JERRY SEINFELD

Simon and Schuster

NEW YORK   LONDON   TORONTO
SYDNEY   NEW DELHI

Simon & Schuster
1230 Avenue of the Americas
New York, NY 10020

First Simon & Schuster hardcover edition October 2020

SIMON & SCHUSTER and colophon are registered trademarks
of Simon & Schuster, Inc.

For information about special discounts for bulk purchases,
please contact Simon & Schuster Special Sales at 1-866-506-1949
or business@simonandschuster.com.

The Simon & Schuster Speakers Bureau can bring authors to your
live event. For more information or to book an event, contact
the Simon & Schuster Speakers Bureau at 1-866-248-3049
or visit our website at www.simonspeakers.com.

Text design by Paul Dippolito

Manufactured in the United States of America

1   3   5   7   9   10   8   6   4   2

Library of Congress Cataloging-in-Publication Data Applied For

ISBN 978-1-9821-1269-1
ISBN 978-1-9821-1274-5 (ebook)

Illustration credits: 1, courtesy of the author;
81, Carson Entertainment Group; 205, courtesy of the author;
251, Kevin Mazur; 353, Jason Sheldon.

Contents

IS
THIS
ANYTHING?

The
Seventies

"Is this anything?" is what every comedian says to every other comedian about any new bit.

Ideas that come from nowhere and mean nothing.

But in the world of stand-up comedy, literal bars of gold.

You see that same comedian later and you will be asked,

"Did it get anything?"

All comedians are slightly amazed when anything works.

Picture me in the mid-1960s, living room floor, legs crossed, bowl of cereal,

one foot from our twenty-five-inch Zenith measured diagonally, jeans, horizontal-stripe T-shirt,

white, low-top US Keds, staring at a comedian in a dark suit and tie on

The Ed Sullivan Show.

I could say something funny once in a while but everything out of this guy's mouth is hilarious.

"How are they able to talk like that?"

I was so mystified and fascinated by them.

But I never, ever imagined I could be one of them.

They were like astronauts or Olympic athletes to me.

Some different, other breed of humans.

Not even really part of the world.

———

I grew up on Long Island and remember, sometime in the early seventies, hearing my friend Chris Misiano's older brother, Vince, say that there was a place in New York City where young people were getting onstage and doing a new kind of stand-up comedy.

That there was a guy who would tell a story while playing a conga drum, and then he started crying and playing the drum in rhythm to the crying!

That sounded so crazy and hilarious to us.

We thought, "We have to see this guy!"

So we started going into the city, which was incredibly fun and exciting anyway, to see these new comedians at the Improv and Catch a Rising Star.

That comedian, of course, was Andy Kaufman.

And there were lots of other amazing comedians there too.

Like Ed Bluestone, Elayne Boosler, Richard Lewis, Bob Shaw, and Bobby Kelton.

We even saw big stars performing at these places, like Rodney Dangerfield and David Brenner.

Hearing live laughs burst out of these crowds in these packed little rooms was almost a scary sound.

How did the comedians know that what they said would get such huge laughs from a crowd of total strangers?

I could not figure it out.

Then in 1974, two things happened that tripped my head out of whatever thick, suburban haze I was in and off into a whole different realm of life.

I read a book called *The Last Laugh* and saw a movie called *Lenny*.

The Last Laugh by Phil Berger was the first book completely about the world of stand-up comedy.

Lenny was a Dustin Hoffman movie about the life of Lenny Bruce.

The poster for *Lenny* showed him in a smoky nightclub hunched over a microphone.

There's a scene in the movie where Lenny Bruce is having dinner late at night in a cafeteria after a show that did not go well.

Tie undone, still in his suit, he pushes his tray along and meets a stripper, Hot Honey Harlowe.

I think that was the scene that did it.

The absolute lack of glamour and/or normalcy drove me wild.

What a completely offbeat, nonsensical existence.

Comedians seemed to hurtle through space and time untethered to anything but the sound of a laugh.

I thought, "Oh my god.

I want to do that.

But—

What if I can't?

What if I'm not funny?"

I remember thinking,

"Well, but I wouldn't have to be that funny anyway.

I would just have to be funny enough to buy a loaf of Wonder bread and a jar of Skippy peanut butter a week."

I could easily survive on that.

It was all I ate in my parents' house, anyway.

And even if that's all I had, it would be a better life than any other I could envision.

I was more than happy to accept being a not-that-funny comedian over any other conceivable option.

Without realizing it, of course, this attitude is the exact right way to start out in the world of comedy.

Expect nothing. Accept anything.

I had only ever tried to make my friends laugh.

That wasn't that easy.

How in the world do you make people that don't even know you laugh?

In *The Last Laugh* I read about a joke Jimmie Walker did at Catch a Rising Star one night.

How great is that name for a nightclub of new comedians, by the way?

Still the best name I've ever heard.

And still the coolest club I ever walked into.

I love that it's the very first place I ever stepped on a stage to try and do comedy.

Anyway, Jimmie Walker's joke was that it was raining so hard in New York that night he "just saw Superman getting into a cab."

I thought that joke was so simple but so funny.

How do you think of something like that?

It just seemed like a miracle to me.

I still don't know exactly for sure where jokes come from.

I think it's from some emotional cocktail of boredom, aggression, intense visual acuity and a kind of Silly Putty of the mind that enables you to re-form what you see into what you want it to be.

I was a very, very nervous performer when I first began going onstage.

But I was encouraged by my Queens College friends Jesse Michnik, Joe Bacino and Mike Costanza.

I am still grateful to those guys.

I was not a naturally outgoing person or really even attention seeking in my normal personality.

My favorite thing was to whisper something funny in class to the kid next to me and crack him up so he got in trouble.

I tried being in a couple plays in high school and college but unless the part was all comedy I couldn't stay interested in the scenes.

I was also reprimanded several times for trying to make a part funny that wasn't supposed to be.

Loved doing that.

Even in the early years of *Seinfeld* I had difficulty focusing on the story aspects of the show.

I would only perk up when Larry and I got to writing the dialogue and we needed funny lines for the characters to say.

I got better at story structure as the years went on but still find that kind of work a bit dreary.

But at twenty years old, when I walked into the Manhattan comedy clubs for the first time, every neuron in my little brain just lit up.

I felt like I had finally found my home on planet Earth.

And it wasn't just that I could now immerse myself in the art of comedy, it was also the world of comedians I was suddenly in.

I have many great friends who are actors, writers and artists of various kinds.

But when I'm in the company of other stand-up comedians I feel like I'm rolling around in a litter of puppies.

―――――

To this day, I feel that same excitement when I walk into a comedy club.

And I have to say, part of it is also this feeling that wherever comedians are working, it is a place of battle.

I am totally in love with the very clear winning-and-losing outcome that a stand-up set can have.

In some ways, it's more sports than theater, really.

This might work tonight.

And it might not.

The real problem of stand-up, of course, is that you must constantly justify why you are the only one talking while a room full of people sit quietly.

And in the beginning, to just put yourself into what is—let's face it—that fairly untenable position, you have to love it badly, madly, maybe even sadly.

Getting live laughs is a druggy kind of lifestyle.

Adrenaline, dopamine, oxytocin.

The drugstore of the brain does not ask if you have a prescription.

It's like those yogurt places where they let you pull the handle yourself.

Oxytocin is sometimes known as "the love drug" because the brain releases it when it receives positive social and/or amorous stimulation.

And let me tell you, when you're on a stage all by yourself

under a hot light,

with a hot mic,

and those laughs are crashing down around you,

it's a strong, pure hit of every addiction you've ever wanted.

When I was young, I was obsessed with race-car driving, big-wave surfing, skydiving

and really fast motorcycles.

One year into doing stand-up comedy I lost interest in all of it.

I learned very quickly that stand-up comedy survival has a lot to do with how much and how good your material is.

I never met a stand-up who wasn't funny at all.

But for the most part, it was the people who killed themselves to keep coming up with great new material who were able to keep rising through the many levels.

And whenever I came up with a funny bit, whether it happened on a stage, in a conversation or working it out on my preferred canvas, the big yellow legal pad, I kept it in one of those old-school accordion folders.

So, I have everything I thought was worth saving from forty-five years of hacking away at this for all I was worth.

And I know for sure it was because I loved doing it so much that I was able to spend endless amounts of time on some of the silliest ideas you can imagine.

And they're all here.

———

Looking back, I like that I was successful.

I'm happy I made money at it.

But honestly, I swear I have really been in it for the laughs since day one, day two and every other day, including today.

I still go out to the clubs every week.

Still love working on the bits.

And appreciate every set I get to do.

And I still get excited meeting and talking to the other stand-up comedians that live for this peculiar, precarious existence.

It was my agent Christian Carino that convinced me people would like to see all this stuff and that we should put it out as a book.

A lot of people I've talked to seemed surprised that I've kept all these notes.

I don't understand why they think that.

I don't understand why I've kept anything else.

What could possibly be of more value?

―――

In the sixties and seventies they would say on TV about certain comedians,

"And he writes all his own stuff."

Because that was a new thing.

Comedians like Bob Hope and Jack Benny would actually joke about their writers as part of their act.

Stand-up comedy in the sixties made the same turn that music did with singer-songwriters becoming the way it was done.

I've never done anything else.

There is something exciting, I think, about being in the same room with the person who originally thought all the ideas you're hearing.

One of my favorite stories about stand-up comics is from my friend Barry Marder.

Barry is a writer, comedian and creator of the Ted L. Nancy character.

In the eighties Barry was making a living selling jokes to comedians at the Comedy Store in LA.

The going rate was $75 a joke.

When Barry's father, a home improvement salesman, heard this, he couldn't believe it.

"Why would they pay that much for a joke?" he asked.

Barry told him,

"Because the guys that need them, *really* need them."

And we do.

I can personally guarantee you that every comedian you've ever seen feels inside that they don't have as much good material as they really wish they had.

The biggest comedians you can name still go onstage with a little worry in the back of their head, that whatever they have might not be good enough tonight.

We always want more.

I deeply love the endless, somewhat torturous struggle of never quite feeling that you've got your act where you want it.

Because I don't want it to ever end.

And when a new bit breaks through and gets a real laugh,

that's when you feel like you're at the beginning of the journey all over again.

You feel like you're just starting out.

And maybe you do have what it takes.

I love hearing a laugh that's never existed in the world before.

Because every laugh is slightly different. Unique even.

So these pages are the map of the forty-five-year-long road I've been on to become this odd, unusual thing that is the only thing I ever really wanted to be.

And I wish I could recommend it to you as an experience you should have.

But it's like recommending that someone become an iguana.

If you don't have those crazy eyes, leathery skin and the long tongue, it's tough to get there.

———

But I hope you enjoy taking the ride that has been my life with me through these pages.

I'm a little frustrated that if you do laugh at something in here I won't get to hear it.

And that's why I'll probably be out at a club in front of an audience somewhere tonight.

"Because the guys that need them, *really* need them."

The Left Bit

I'm left-handed.

Left-handed people do not like that the word "left"

is so often associated

with negative things.

Two left feet.

Left-handed compliment.

Bad ideas are always "out of left field."

What are we having for dinner?

Leftovers.

You go to a party, nobody's there.

"Where'd everybody go?"

"They left."

Bumper Cars

Another exciting day in my childhood was when we got to go on the Bumper Cars.

You really find out what you're made of on the Bumper Cars.

A brutal contest of man and machine.

Driving as an act of pure hostility.

All confrontation, no destination.

Except, when the ride starts there's always one kid stuck in a pack of empty cars.

Can't get out.

This is the same guy you see later on with the attendant hanging off the back helping him steer.

I always feel bad when I hit somebody I don't know.

Feels too much like a real accident.

I get out, exchange registrations.

Inspect the damage.

There's always some guy a little too into it.

Lives for the sensation of impact.

You'll see this guy with saliva on his chin.

As he puts a helpless father-and-son team through a wall.

Cotton Balls

I like women.

Although, I find their bathrooms one of the most frightening places in the world.

I don't even want to see what happens when they crank up some of that equipment.

You have that makeup mirror.

With the aircraft landing lights on either side.

The rows of hot curlers in that plastic thing.

Do you put those in with your hands or do you just launch them right out of the box?

Like little cruise curlers.

I suppose once you got the curlers in your hair,

you can cook potatoes on those things sticking up.

Lot of cotton balls in there too.

Women use a lot of cotton balls.

A LOT of cotton balls.

The thing I don't understand is, I have never needed a cotton ball.

Never.

Not one.

We're both human beings.

What's going on?

I've never wanted a cotton ball.

Never bought a cotton ball.

Never had a cotton ball.

Never been in a situation where I thought to myself,

"I could use a cotton ball right now.

I could certainly get out of this mess."

Women need them.

And they don't need one or two.

They need thousands of them every single day.

They buy these bags, they're like peat moss bags.

Big steel straps around them.

They have them dropped on the front lawn with a fork lift.

Two days later, they're all out.

They're on their way back to the store to buy more cotton balls.

The only time I ever see them,

there's always 2 or 3 in the bottom of your little waste basket

that look like they've been through some horrible experience.

Tortured, interrogated.

I don't know what you did to them.

A woman once left 3 cotton balls over my house.

Took me a year to get rid of them.

I put one on the floor of my kitchen.

I thought maybe the cockroaches would see it.

Think it's a tumbleweed and go,

"This is a dead town, let's move on."

Or, I'd go to the doctor.

Before they give you the shot,

they put the alcohol on your arm with a cotton ball.

And when he went for his, I'd go,

"Maybe you could use this one?

Come on, Doc, give me a break.

I'm just trying to use them up."

Sometimes he'd use it.

Take a penny off on my bill.

Then he gives me the prescription.

I take that home.

Open up the bottle.

There's another cotton ball in there.

The Cotton Ball Syndicate was always one step ahead.

Dogs in Cars

I love taking my dog out in my car.

Lot of trouble in the turns, though.

Doesn't understand inertia.

Legs get all tense and quivery.

"What's happening here . . . ? What's going on?"

He doesn't know whether to stand up, sit down.

Dogs like the car because from the outside it looks like a regular person sitting next to you.

They feel equal.

They look over,

"This is nice.

This is more like it.

I think we should sit together like this all the time."

Then every turn he just drops out of view.

Until he can get back up again.

I don't know why dogs always stick their head out the window.

I think they think,

"If I could run this fast, I'd be King of the Dogs."

If you take your dog out into the world, it amazes them the things that you can do.

Any time of the day you get hungry, you can stop somewhere, come out with a hamburger.

This blows their mind.

They look at you with the expression,

"Where did you get that . . . ?

It's not 5:30.

It's the middle of the day.

How'd you get fed?

That thing you are eating is the greatest thing I have ever seen."

The real difference between man and animal is one thing, pockets.

It's not opposable thumbs.

It's pockets.

Dogs dig holes in the ground because they're trying to make pockets.

This is what has held the animal kingdom back.

You may say,

"Then why hasn't the kangaroo advanced as a species? They've got pockets."

They do.

But they've got those short little arms, they can't reach the pockets.

"I have money to buy things.

I just can't get to it."

Life Cereal

Arrogance.

Too much arrogance.

Everywhere.

Even the food industry.

Where in the world do you get your balls

to call a breakfast cereal LIFE?

What do they see in their little square oat cereal

that makes them think that it should be named after our very existence?

"How about Oaties, Squaries, Brownies?"

"Oh no, this is much bigger than that.

This is LIFE, I tell you.

It's LIFE."

What other names you think they considered?

How about "Almighty God"?

Was that in the running?

Who wouldn't want to wake up in the morning to a nice big bowl of "Almighty God"?

Or New, "Almighty God With Raisins."

And if you don't like it,

you can go to hell.

Parakeet Mirror

My mother would always talk to me about what she's going to do with the living room.

This was her obsession.

She was gonna fix the living room.

"I want to change the living room."

My mother would say,

"You know, if you make one wall of a room a mirror

people think you have an entire other room."

She believed this.

What kind of an idiot walks up to a mirror and goes,

"Hey look, there's a whole other room in there.

There's a guy in there that looks just like me."

My parakeet would fall for this.

I would let him out of his cage.

He would fly around and he would go "BANG" right into the mirror.

With his little head that was very smooth at the front.

And the feathers would fly.

And he'd hit the ground.

Then he'd fly off in another direction a little askew.

But even if he thinks the mirror is another room,

why doesn't he at least try and avoid hitting the OTHER parakeet?

"Look—up!"

What happened to bird's-eye view and all that?

There's another parakeet coming right at you!

Roosevelt Island Tramway

I see they just finished the Roosevelt Island Tramway.

That's nice . . .

The city's going bankrupt,

they're putting up rides for us.

Next thing you know, there'll be a roller coaster through the South Bronx.

That would be the first roller coaster where the people scream on the flat part of the ride.

Superman TV Show

For me,

when I was a kid,

I thought the Superman TV show was probably the greatest TV show there's ever been.

Have you ever seen a rerun?

You go, "What was I, out of my mind for a half hour every day?"

There is not one believable microsecond in this entire series.

The Daily Planet. The newspaper.

Largest circulation newspaper in the entire city.

They had three reporters.

Each week two of them are tied up in a cave somewhere.

I always wanted Superman to one time tell Lois and Jimmy,

"Look, you're not helping. You're only making my job harder.

Would you both please just let me deal with crooks?

Believe me, I can handle it."

Superman and Clark Kent are the same person.

But no one knows because of the secret identity.

The disguise?

A pair of glasses.

That's it.

No other difference in these two faces.

Jimmy Olsen and Lois Lane. Professional journalists.

Able to observe and analyze every detail of their environment.

They see no resemblance.

These are two entirely different people to their trained eye.

If a friend of yours gets new glasses . . .

is it impossible to recognize them?

Clark Kent didn't even have lenses in the frames of the glasses.

He would scratch his eye right through them.

So, Clark Kent wears the Super costume underneath the business suit.

We've seen him tear open the shirt.

What about the Superman boots?

They go inside the regular shoes? How does that work?

"I see Clark's got those red leather socks on again today."

Did Jimmy Olsen ever get suspicious seeing Clark Kent in the men's room?

(Peeing in classic Superman "fists on waist" pose)

Dogs Vote

I'm looking forward to being an old man.

I have to.

I can't look back on it.

Parents always like to blow you away with their "the way it used to be" stories.

"Milk was a nickel. Car was a quarter."

And I always think, could the world possibly change that much again?

So that we will have equally amazing stories . . .

I wonder if young people will ever say things to us like,

"Grandpa, you mean when you were a kid, no dogs could vote?"

"That's right, Jimmy.

They had no say in the world at all.

They were just pets."

"Woww . . ."

Disneyland

I never went to Disneyland as a child.

That was never going to happen.

My parents were not taking me to a different state,

thousands of miles away, so I could sit in a teacup.

My mother and father were both orphans.

Their attitude was,

"You have a room. You have a bed. That's your ride."

I couldn't even speak the word.

"Mom, Dad, there's a place called Dis—"

"What?"

"Dis—. . . Dis-nuh . . ."

That was the most I could get out.

Dad's Thermostat

You can't beat Adult Power.

Unlimited television.

Cookies any time you want.

Plus you can go home tonight and screw around with that thermostat all you like.

We are in charge of it now.

My father got me so crazy with that thing.

I didn't go near a thermostat until I was 28 years old.

I was in a hotel room in Pittsburgh when I finally got up the guts to move it a little bit.

The whole night I couldn't sleep.

I was afraid my father was going to burst in the door,

"Who touched the thermostat in here?

You know, I set it there . . . for a reason."

For years I waited for my father to take me aside

and explain to me the secret of the thermostat.

And then one day he did sit me down,

told me this whole story—

The sperm, the egg, intercourse.

I said, "Dad, who cares?

Get to the part where the thermostat comes in.

What does it really control?"

Parents Look Like

I'm wearing contact lenses now but I wore glasses at the age of 10.

I thought I had to get glasses because I couldn't tell what my parents looked like.

I'd ask my mother for money and she'd always say,

"What do I look like, a bank?"

"Do I look like I'm made of money to you?"

The truth is, when you're a kid your parents are the bank.

Where else am I going to get money?

Am I going to walk into Chase Manhattan?

They're going to say,

"What do I look like, your mother?"

"Beat it, four eyes . . ."

Adult Pockets

One big difference between adults and kids is

the number of pockets they go through when they're looking for something.

Adults touch every pocket on their clothes when they're looking for something.

"I thought . . . for sure . . . I had . . . that with me . . ."

When you're a little kid,

somebody asks you if you have something,

you just hold both palms straight out.

"No, I don't have it."

You don't have to check.

You have nothing.

Anything you have is in your hand.

You ask a kid, "You have change of a quarter?"

(hold hands out palms up)

He goes, "Nope."

Ask him to double-check, "Are you sure?"

They just spread their fingers out wider.

Pajamas

I don't know why the suit projects this image of power.

Why is it intimidating?

"We'd better do what this guy says, his pants match his jacket."

Men love the suit so much, we've actually styled our pajamas to look like a tiny suit.

Three buttons down the front.

The little lapels.

Breast pocket.

What's that for?

You put a pencil in there.

Roll over in the middle of the night.

You kill yourself.

Ruin Appetite

I really wanted adulthood at a certain point.

I just couldn't build one more balsa wood glider.

I needed it to be over.

I needed it to be:

If I want a cookie,

I have a cookie.

I will have 3 cookies.

6 cookies.

Or 8 cookies, if I want.

Sometimes in fact,

I will intentionally ruin my entire appetite.

Because as adults we understand . . .

Even if you ruin an appetite,

there's another appetite coming right behind it.

There's no danger of running out of appetites.

I can ruin 100 of them.

Still have thousands left.

Why are we being so careful with each one?

I got millions of appetites.

The Frigidaire Building

The best toy I ever had as a kid was when somebody on our street got a new refrigerator,

and I got that big brown cardboard box to play with.

Because as a kid,

this is the closest you're going to come to having your own apartment.

You crawl in, "I think I'll just live here from now on."

Cut a hole for a window, stick your head out.

"Mom, Dad, you must come over some time.

We live so close.

I'm on the front lawn.

It's the Frigidaire building.

Apartment #1."

First Wallet

I remember my first wallet.

The brown plastic one with the little cowboy on it.

It's the only wallet where you take the time to fill out the I.D. card that comes with the wallet.

Because you need identification when you're seven years old.

In case they check you getting on the merry-go-round.

"Yeah, I'm old enough for the zebra . . . that's me.

I don't know about these other kids,

but I've got the card already filled out."

Jawbreakers

Must be fun inventing new candy for kids.

The nutritional leeway is unbelievable.

We had candy called JAWBREAKERS.

Candy so hard, it was conceivable you could break your jaw trying to eat it.

We thought this was great.

Kids never go,

"Hey, what's in this product?

Jimmy, let me check the ingredients in these Jawbreakers.

Artificial coloring isn't the best thing to put in our system, you know."

Kids think,

"Only 25¢ for a chance at serious injury?

That's good value."

Shoe Store Walk

I think shoes are one of the toughest things to buy.

You just look in the window of a shoe store . . .

You can see people having a tough time.

Brows furrowed . . .

Just staring off into the distance.

Why when we try on a new pair of shoes and walk around the store, do we have this vacant zombie look?

(walking around slowly)

"Yeah . . . these . . . feel . . . pretty . . . good . . ."

Your brain is so focused on your feet there's none left to operate your face.

"Are these the 9 . . . ?

Or the 9½ . . . ?

I . . . just . . . can't . . . seem . . . to . . . feel . . . my . . . feet . . ."

Some shoes come in different widths.

Some don't.

So . . .

Do we need different widths or don't we?

Then you go over to that little one-foot-high mirror on the floor.

So you can see the shoes from your cat's POV.

Or if I walk past a drunk lying on the street,

"What do you think of these?

I happen to know they look very good from that angle."

Cub Scouts

I was a Cub Scout when I was 9 years old.

Any ex-Cubbies here . . . ?

Anyone still go to the meetings?

It's tough to stay with it.

But it stays with you.

When you've had a little yellow button on top of your head you never forget.

I remember I'd get the outfit all set up, blue pants, blue shirt, little yellow neckerchief.

That giant metal thing to hold the neckerchief together.

You go outside, get beat up, come back, put your regular clothes on.

You're not making it to school in that outfit.

That's why we formed packs.

To survive.

It's also why they taught us to camp in the wilderness.

If we had normal clothes we'd check into a hotel like anybody else.

In that getup you want to be in the woods.

I spent 99% of my time as a Cub Scout just trying to get my hat back.

That was all I did.

Running back and forth at my bus stop going, "Quit it . . . !"

I think the first merit badge book was "Bear," then "Lion."

I never got past "Bear."

I thought,

"Bear, Lion, at this rate we'll never get to women."

Even at 9 I was thinking,

"Come on, nightclubs, birth control, pick up the pace.

I'm not meeting a lot of bears out there."

Swiss Army Knife

The Swiss Army.

Never been involved in a war in two hundred years.

It's a lucky thing.

Did you ever see this little Swiss Army knife?

Corkscrews, bottle openers, nail file.

You don't want to go to war with this thing.

Unless they're in the war of the Dinner Parties they have no chance.

"Come on, buddy, let's go . . .

You get past me, the guy behind me has a spoon.

I got the toenail clippers out, so just back off.

I'll clip that pinky toe down to nothing.

Take you three weeks to grow it back."

Gym Class

Health clubs should be like gym class.

Make everybody wear the little same color gym suit.

Remember your gym suit?

"Where's your suit? You can't take gym without your suit."

It was like a suit.

Top and bottom same material.

Jockstrap.

It's a three-piece suit.

Strong elastic on those gym shorts.

And those little pant legs that just came straight out.

Really flatters the powerful physique most boys have at 11
years old.

Toothpick legs.

Bell-bottom shorts.

I never washed my gym suit either.

Not once.

What for?

Is it going to look better?

Get compliments from the other guys in my squad?

"Nice, is that the gray medium? Sharp."

I think one killer thing for everybody in gym class was
The Rope.

What was that about?

It didn't fit in with the whole rest of the little fitness program,
did it?

Few jumping jacks, little volleyball, and then North Vietnam
POW escape training.

"Come on, get up that rope."

"Coach, do I need to practice this? I don't think I'm ever going
to date Rapunzel."

Remember that big knot on the bottom of the rope?

That's in case you lose your grip at the top, the knot stops you
before you hit the ground.

Six inches between the knot and the floor, that's your safety
zone.

And if you ever did slide down the rope,

they could cook marshmallows from the flames coming off
your thighs.

What kind of rope was that?

It was like from a Spanish pirate ship.

Some kind of super-heat friction twine?

Did they do tests?

"No, we're not getting enough redness and inflammation from this type of rope.

We need something with like little spiny things coming out the sides."

75% Body Heat

I was reading this article about how to dress for cold weather.

And they said that 75% of all body heat is lost through the top of the head.

Which sounds like you could go skiing naked if you got a good hat.

Parent Boss

The best job security is the jobs you do as a kid around the house.

You cannot lose that job.

No matter how bad you did.

I knew my father's not going to call me in the house,

"Listen, son, you're not really cutting the mustard out there on that lawn.

Now, I know you've been our son for 15 years.

But I'm afraid we're going to have to let you go.

Don't feel bad.

We're making cutbacks all over the house.

The dog's only coming in 3 days a week.

He missed a couple Frisbees at the picnic.

We had to trim his hours."

Mom's Walls

My mother's very into walls.

Always looking at walls.

Thinking about walls.

Working on walls.

Always wants my opinion.

"What do you think about this wall?

I'm thinking about changing it.

How about mauve?

What do you think?"

"I don't know, Mom.

I don't think about walls.

To me, if it's forcing you to use the door to get out of the room, it's working."

Then we'd have to go to the wallpaper store and she'd look through these huge wallpaper books.

Giant books with huge pages.

They're like the Koran.

Each page is 3 feet.

It's a religious experience for her.

"Whooosh . . . Yes. I see what they're saying."

I would get so bored I couldn't pick up my feet.

"When can we get out of here?"

That's what happens when you're a kid.

There's a level of boredom where you cannot support your body weight.

My parents would take me to the bank and I would just liquefy.

I'd walk in,

"Oh, I can't handle this . . ."

The legs just give out.

They'd turn around from the teller's window and I would be flat on my back in the middle of the floor.

Out cold from boredom.

How many times did your parents have to say to you, "Would you get up off the floor?"

"I can't. I'm so bored."

They do that scream whisper,

"I said, GET UP . . ."

They would grab your arm to try and pick you up, and you would just twirl around the floor like cooked spaghetti.

"I can't get up, Mom.

I'm so sorry.

I have no bones anymore from the boredom of this bank."

Adulthood is the ability to be totally bored and remain standing.

Supermarket line, Motor Vehicle Bureau.

You hang right in there, solid as a rock.

Skydive at 19

I went skydiving once.

I was 19.

Horrible thing to do to your parents.

They've just spent 19 years trying to protect me from harm, injury, disease.

I turn around,

"Mom, Dad, it's a pretty nice day . . .

What do you say we risk the whole ball of wax right now?

My idea is this,

I go up in a plane thousands of feet in the air.

Hurl myself out.

Attempt to operate the parachute correctly.

And avoid plummeting to an almost certain death.

. . . Can you lend me the 75 bucks?"

Red Metal Horses

The only thing they had for kids when I was out with my parents

was sometimes on the sidewalk they'd have like two red metal horses.

It wasn't really a ride.

It was like a ride fragment that somehow chipped off of a real ride.

Nobody went "wheee" on these things.

It would just kind of grind back and forth for 45 seconds.

It felt like a motor from a grain elevator.

Like you were milling buckwheat.

But compared to lying on the floor of the bank it was Space Mountain to me.

I get off, "Mom, I feel 1,000% better after that.

I'm refreshed.

I'm calm.

I'm ready for the wallpaper store again.

You want to go back there?

Guest towels. Throw pillows. Drapery.

I'm into all of it."

Skydiving Helmet

Skydiving is definitely the scariest thing I've done.

My question,

what exactly is the point of the helmet?

Can you "kind of" make it?

I think if you jump out of a plane,

and that chute doesn't open,

the *helmet* is now wearing *you* for protection.

Later on, the helmet's talking with the other helmets going,

"It's a good thing he was there or I would've hit the ground directly.

You never jump out of a plane unless you have got a human being strapped underneath you.

That's basic safety."

Scuba Dying

Learned to scuba dive last year.

Another great, fun sport where your main activity is to "not-die."

(singing)

"Don't die . . . don't die, don't die, don't die . . .

There's a fish, there's a rock, who cares? Don't die . . .

I don't want to die. Don't let me die.

Let's swim and breathe and live.

Because living is good and dying is bad . . ."

You die, that's scuba dying.

It's a whole different sport.

A lot less equipment.

Just grab a cinder block and jump in.

I went and got a waterproof wallet.

In case I run into a sea turtle that can break a fifty, I guess . . .

I got a waterproof watch.

That's important.

"Well, I'm completely out of oxygen and look-at-the-time.

Now, I'm dead AND I'm late."

Sister Married

I have an older sister who's married.

It was hard at first but I've adjusted to it now.

When a brother or a sister tells you they're getting married it's a shock,

because the way you know them,

you can't believe anyone would marry them.

I met the guy,

I said,

"Let me get this straight.

You intentionally want to spend the rest of your life with my sister?

I have to tell you,

I've done what you want to do.

It's a big mistake.

Have you ever tried to borrow a record album from her?

Ever shared the back seat on a long car trip?

You're going to need an imaginary line.

NO ONE'S ALLOWED TO CROSS IT."

Coming Out to My Parents

My parents never knew I was funny growing up.

I don't know why but I was very embarrassed to show them that side of myself.

I'll never forget how incredibly nervous I was bringing them to my show the first time.

I had my little gay closet moment.

"Mom, Dad, I don't know how else to say this, but . . . I'm funny.

I'm a funny person.

I've always been funny.

It's who I am.

I don't want to be ashamed of it anymore.

I want to lead a funny lifestyle.

I want to have breakfast at 2 in the afternoon with other funny people."

And I was out.

Father Sofa

Fathers like when you visit.

He's always got some heavy thing he's been waiting 3 weeks to move.

"Hey, look who's here. Give me a hand with this."

My father would never move a sofa unless he had a cigarette in his mouth.

Burned down to about a quarter-inch long.

With the smoke going right in the eye.

"You got your end? (cough)

You got it?

Your end has got to come around . . . (cough)

You got it?"

Because you want your eyes blinking and tearing

when you're walking backwards down a staircase holding a wall unit.

That's the easy way to do it.

That was his other big advice when we're moving something.

"Easy . . . easy."

What does that mean?

"Easy, easy, easy."

It's not easy.

It's very difficult.

You should be saying,

"DIFFICULT . . . DIFFICULT . . . DIFFICULT . . .

EXTREMELY DIFFICULT.

IMPOSSIBLE. IMPOSSIBLE.

PUT IT DOWN. PUT IT DOWN. PUT IT DOWN.

IT'S IMPOSSIBLE."

At least be honest.

You want easy?

Let's leave it here in the hallway.

That's easy.

Toilet Roll with a Hat

I come from the kind of family where

my mother kept an extra roll of toilet paper on the tank of the toilet

and it had a little knit hat with a pom-pom on it.

I didn't know if it was so people wouldn't know that we had an extra roll of toilet paper

or because my mother felt even toilet paper is embarrassed to be what it is.

But the toilet paper had a hat, the dog had a sweater,

and the couch arms had little fabric toupees.

I think it might be why recreational drugs never interested me growing up.

Reality was trippy enough.

The Parakeet Life

To me, the ultimate would be to live the Parakeet Lifestyle.

It's the most efficient apartment possible.

A well-ventilated room overlooking the paper.

Don't even have to walk to the bathroom.

Toilet and newspaper are already combined.

Food and water mounted on the wall.

You want to go to sleep,

turn your head around, put it in your back.

Morning you don't even have to get up,

you're already standing.

Double-check the cage door lock.

See what the cat's up to.

Take the rest of the day off.

Cold Cereal

The most magic words to me as a kid were: FREE INSIDE.

I guess they said that because it would have been a drag to see,

TOY INSIDE. WE'LL BILL YOU LATER.

Didn't matter what the thing was as long as it was FREE INSIDE.

Your mother has to pay $1.29, but to you it's free.

Because all you have to do is dump the cereal out on the counter

and you get a little plastic monkey.

Hangs on the side of the bowl and watches you eat.

Sometimes it would say, MINIATURE REPLICA.

Which was also exciting.

But what is that, really?

It's a tiny fake.

The other thing it would say is, ACTUAL SIZE.

Which meant it was actually the size that it was.

I got this from inside my Fruity Pebbles box.

It's a Fred Flintstone glitter patch.

It's an interesting cross-section of prehistoric and modern times.

Who's into the Flintstones *and* glitter?

Those recipes on the side were always weird.

I don't know why I could never get my mother to make Cornflakes Cantonese.

I always wanted to have a dinner party and make one of those recipes.

Invite people.

Get them all seated.

Roll out a serving table.

Then lift up a sterling silver cover on Cocoa Peanut Logs Parmigiana.

Grape-Nuts

Grape-Nuts is a mysterious product.

You open the box,

pour it in the bowl,

no grapes,

no nuts.

What's the story?

Can you call things anything you want now?

Can you call "milk," "shoes"?

You open the carton.

Pour it on your feet.

"Hey, these aren't shoes . . .

What the hell is this . . . ?"

Cereal Serving Suggestion

On the front of cereal boxes they always have that perfect picture.

And for some reason it always has to say right next to it, "Serving suggestion."

Like,

"We're not insisting on a bowl.

Just a suggestion . . .

Put it in your hat if you want . . .

Milk?

Just another idea . . .

Putting it out there.

Throw it up in the air.

Run under it with your mouth open . . .

We don't care.

It's your business.

We suggest,

MILK.

In a *bowl.*

With a *spoon.*

But, just to be clear . . .

we only suggested it.

Somebody gets hurt, it's not our fault."

Cookie Crisp

Our parents had no clue there was no food in any of these products.

Until the Cookie Crisp people came along and blew the lid off the whole racket.

Just one little step too far . . .

Cookie Crisp should have been called,

"The Hell wth Everything."

This is a cereal that . . .

it's not *like* cookies, it *is* cookies.

This is your breakfast, a bowl of chocolate chip cookies.

Ice cream for lunch, cake for dinner, bacon and cigarettes in between.

This is the Cookie Crisp Total Health Plan.

I think it was after a bowl of Cookie Crisp that Nietzsche said,

"If it doesn't kill you, it makes you stronger."

Void Where Prohibited

There's a lot of scary things on cereal boxes to a kid.

"Void where prohibited" used to scare me a lot.

Whenever there was an offer to send away for something,

on the back of the box it would always say,

"Void Where Prohibited."

So, how do you know if your house is in a prohibited zone?

Your father's got to drive you over the state line so you can play with it.

Like, a battery-operated plastic frogman.

He sits in the car waiting for you.

"Hurry up and play with it. We've got to get home."

"I'm hurrying."

Proof of Purchase

Proof-of-purchase seal seems like another overly serious terminology for a box of cereal.

"Proof of Purchase."

"Prove it."

"Freeze. Whose cereal is this?"

What happened with just sending in box tops?

Are they getting too many forgeries down at Kellogg's?

"Jim, run these Cocoa Puff lids through the infrared scanner one more time.

I've got a gut feeling about this Tommy Wilson kid.

If he thinks he's going to put it past me again like he did with that Civil War set he's got another thing coming."

Enough Jokes

I guess the big question at this point in the evening is,

when are you people going to leave?

I know, it's a tough thing to decide.

"One more guy?

Let's see if the next one's any good, then we'll leave."

When you're in a restaurant,

you know when you've had enough food.

But when you're in a nightclub how do you know when you've heard enough jokes?

"Ha, ha.

You know what? That's enough for me.

No really, thank you.

I'm full.

Not another routine.

I'm stuffed.

I'm serious.

I could not possibly have one more witty aside or clever remark.

I've really had more than enough."

Parents Comedians?

People do say strange things to you when you come offstage.

Someone once said to me,

"Hey, you were really funny.

Were your parents comedians?"

"Yes, and all my relatives are comedians.

Every single member of my family is a working, professional stand-up comic.

You ought to come over at Thanksgiving.

It's a riot.

When I was 5 all the other kids were playing with toys.

My parents gave me a tuxedo and a pinky ring."

Sock Closet

When you buy socks they always come on a tiny hanger.

Does anybody have a tiny sock closet to hang them up?

Tiny doors.

Go through them to pick out what you're wearing that day.

(fingers going through)

"Argyle . . . crew . . . tube sock . . . over the calf . . ."

The Sock Escape

But the life of The Sock is not good.

We know that.

The stinky feet.

The boring drawers.

They want out.

Laundry day is their only chance to escape.

And they know it.

How many times do you do your laundry?

Go to the dryer.

Count up the socks.

One of them got out.

Escaped.

Where did he go?

Took off on his own.

Never takes his partner.

"This is *my* chance.

I'm tired of everyone thinking we're the same."

The dryer door swings open.

The sock hides himself up against the side wall . . .

(arm feeling around inside)

"I know he's in there . . ."

Sometimes he grabs on to a sweater.

Give him a little head start.

And then he takes off down the street . . .

(chase scene music)

"Da dada . . . Dada dada . . ."

How could one sock even survive in the world?

In what circumstance?

On a golf club?

Puppet show?

Amputee?

There's just not that many options.

Sometimes you'll see *one sock* just lying there in the street . . .

Dirty . . . twisted . . . exhausted.

He only made it a couple of blocks . . .

The Sock Left Behind

And what about the sock that gets left behind?

What are his prospects?

"Oh, so I get thrown out now . . . ?

Because of him?

How is that fair?

What did I do?

The whole drawer knew he was going to pull a stunt like this someday.

Why do you think he was always inside out or rolling down at the top?

He was never really one of us from the beginning."

Smokers Win Arguments

The ultimate conversation prop is the cigarette.

You cannot win an argument with someone that has a cigarette in their hand.

They're always waving it around.

"I've got fire right in front of my face.

See that?

Does that intimidate you in any way?"

———

And then when they put it out, that just ends the argument.

I can go,

"I think this.

I feel this.

My opinion is this."

They go,

"Really?

That's what you think?

(exhale smoke)

Pphhphphph . . .

(twisting toe on the ground)

No.

It's out.

You're wrong."

Vivian Is Back

I saw a sign in a beauty parlor,

"Vivian is back."

From where?

Lunch?

Prison?

It could be anywhere.

I didn't even know she left.

They never had a sign,

"Vivian's on a chain gang in Alabama."

Can't this woman have a private life?

Everyone's got to know where she is?

"Vivian's getting an egg salad on the corner."

"Vivian's making license plates in Coxsacki."

Notary Public

These notary public people seem to think they're pretty something.

With their special little stampers.

"I need to get this notarized."

"Well, the notary isn't here right now.

You'll have to wait.

NO ONE ELSE can do it."

Only The Notary has the power, the skill, the training.

To take a stamper and go,

"Boom—boom"

You ever want to just grab it out of his hand and go,

"There, I have the power now!

You see?

He's just a man!

(holding it out like a ray gun)

Back . . . everyone back."

I'm going to bring my own stamper next time.

With just a huge *OK* on it.

Stamp everything on his desk.

"There, now your stuff's approved by me."

What kind of course you have to go through to become part of this elite corps anyway?

Some class where the teacher stands at the front and goes,

"Alright, everyone. Ready . . . and . . .

Stamp and press and hold and up . . .

And . . . BACK to the pad.

And press, and stamp

Rock it on the pad, rock it on the pad.

and hold and up

And . . . BACK to the pad.

And . . . breathe . . .

Higgins, you're not breathing.

Alright, alright, shake it off, everyone, shake it off.

That was very good stamping."

Lobster Tank

Then you have the attitude toward a creature like the lobster.

It's not enough that we want to catch them, kill them and eat them.

We also want to walk into the restaurant.

See the guy in the tank,

sweating it out.

"Maybe I'll get a hamburger.

(turns sharply)

Maybe . . ."

And they're nervous, you can see it.

They try to stay in the background.

I once saw a lobster in a pair of overalls.

He was cleaning the inside of the tank.

(scrubbing)

"I just work here.

I'm not on the menu."

All the other lobsters were laughing at him.

"Go ahead and laugh.

I've been here nine years."

Piano Store

Every mall I have ever been in has a piano store.

I have never seen anybody in there buying one.

You go to the mall, you've got $20, $30.

You buy a book, a pair of jeans.

You ever see anybody go,

"Hey, before we leave, let's pick up one of those pianos!

What are they, like, A MILLION DOLLARS . . . ?

Let's get it now so we don't have to make two trips."

Visual Security

I have a friend that was worried about getting his car radio stolen

so he used to put a little towel on the dashboard that hangs over it.

Certainly nothing strikes fear into the heart of the criminal psyche

like the sight of a small dish towel.

Especially if it's got the little fringe on the end.

That really terrifies them.

They run to their secret caves and tremble.

———

We're going to get ripped off.

We think we're not.

Everybody has their own little personal security things.

We think we're going to foil the crooks.

We go to the beach,

go in the water,

put your wallet in the sneaker.

Who's going to know?

What criminal mind could penetrate this Fortress of Security?

"I put it down by the toe.

They never look there.

They check the heels,

they move on."

Or you have a TV set in the back seat of your car,

then you have to leave the car in the street for a few minutes,

so you put a sweater over the TV.

"It's a couple of sweaters, that's all.

One of them happens to be square with antenna coming out of it. It's a Zenith sweater."

Vague

Did you ever write a report or a paper in school,

and you get it back

and the teacher has written "Vague" across a whole page?

It's frustrating.

Because "Vague" is kind of a vague thing to say . . .

I would just write "Unclear," send it back to the teacher.

She'd return it to me, "Ambiguous."

We're still corresponding to this day . . .

Pay Phone Call

The other day I went a little overtime at a pay phone.

I hang up.

As I'm walking away, the phone rings.

It's the phone company.

They want more money.

It's the greatest feeling.

For the first time in your life, you've got them right where you want them.

I always let it ring a few times.

"Hello?

Operator . . . ?

Yes, uh-huh . . . I see

Oh, I've got the money.

I've got the money right here.

TAP, TAP.

Hear that?

That's a quarter.

Yeah, you want that, don't you?

Well, to tell you the truth, I didn't think the connection was that good.

Plus, you interrupted me a couple of times.

I didn't like that.

I'm going to have to think about this whole thing.

Call me back . . .

I don't know, I'll be in the general area.

Ring them all . . ."

Left Turn Okay

The signs directing traffic flow are usually very straight.

"One way."

"Right turn only."

"Wrong Way. Go Back."

I think my favorite is,

"Left turn okay."

That one's got a little personal touch to it.

"Left turn . . . okay."

It's like,

"We're not crazy about you making a left . . .

It's okay.

Believe me, I've seen better."

I think a lot of these signs could loosen up a bit.

"Right turn, why not?"

"U-turn?

Enjoy it!"

Political Mascots

I understand the kind of politicians we have.

They're those people.

That's the way it is.

I comprehend it.

What I don't understand is the mascot animals we ended up with.

The Elephant and the Donkey.

There's only two major parties.

They had the entire animal kingdom to pick from.

"The magnificent black stallion?"

"No."

"Bengal tiger?"

"No."

"Hey, how about a jackass?"

"I like the jackass idea.

I think it's an impressive animal.

And I really like what it says about us."

"You don't think people will think we're jackasses

because we've chosen a jackass as our symbol?"

"I do not.

It's two completely separate and different things."

Republicans went,

"Well, if they're going jackass . . .

Perhaps some sort of big, smelly, slow-witted circus animal.

I know people respect the elephant.

Probably because of that little hat they wear.

When you weigh 5 tons nothing looks better than the smallest possible hat with a chin strap."

———

By the way, another interesting thing about circus elephants.

And this is true.

Before the circus starts, they stick a pole up the elephant's ass . . .

This is to make it go, so it doesn't take a giant crap during the "performance."

Which is certainly the kind of positive image we want for our political party.

I think it says, "We are ready to do whatever we have to do."

Unemployed

Unemployment, that's a tough thing.

Even if you get a job, after you've been unemployed,

they take unemployment out of your check every week and show it to you in that little box.

So every paycheck has the word "unemployment" on it.

You can't get it out of your mind.

You just got the job, they're already getting ready for you to be laid off.

I have a friend who's collecting unemployment insurance.

This guy has never worked so hard in his life to keep this going.

He's down there every week, waiting on the lines,

getting interviewed, making up all these lies about looking for jobs.

If they had any idea of the effort he's making to avoid work,

I'm sure they'd give him a raise.

I've never seen someone do such a tremendous job not working.

The *New York Times*

The first inside page of the *New York Times* is always a strange view of the world.

They always have a full-page glamourous fashion ad.

Right next to the third-world persecution story.

"Wow, in South America political prisoners are being dragged through the streets by their feet,

. . . and I see Saks is having a sale."

"Actually, that *would* be a nice outfit for a beating.

Those would be great loafers for fleeing oppression.

They make a statement and they're comfortable to run in."

Eyewitness News

I watched *Eyewitness News* the other day.

These people apparently saw the whole thing happen themselves.

The entire show it's just 30 minutes of them just holding up Polaroids.

"That's me next to the killer, there."

"Here I am waving from the *back* of the getaway car."

Watching News

Something happens when a man reaches a certain age that

The News becomes the most important thing in his life.

I remember when it happened to my father.

All fathers think one day they're going to get a call from the State Department.

"Listen, we've completely lost track of the situation in the Middle East.

You've been watching the news.

What do you think we should do about it?"

TV Cooking

I will never understand why they cook on TV.

I can't smell it.

Can't eat it.

Can't taste it.

The end of the show they hold it up to the camera.

"Well, here it is.

You can't have any.

Thanks for watching.

Goodbye."

The Prisoners of Inertia

The question you have to ask yourself about professional wrestling is a simple one.

If professional wrestling did not exist, could you come up with this idea?

Could you envision the popularity of huge men in tiny bathing suits pretending to fight?

Could you sell it to a promoter?

"I'm telling you, Sid, millions of people will enjoy this.

Giant guys in tiny suits, and they won't really fight."

It's the only sport where participants are just thrown right out into the audience

and no one in the crowd thinks anything unusual is happening.

If you're watching golf and Arnold Palmer goes flying over your head . . .

First of all, I would say you're watching a very competitive tournament.

And how about the professional wrestling referee?

There's a great job.

You're a referee in a sport with no rules of any kind.

How do you screw that up?

The referee is kind of like Larry of the Three Stooges.

You don't really need him, it just wouldn't be the same without him.

They must get these guys from the same place the Harlem Globetrotters get their refs.

There must be this whole school where they teach you

to just kind of run around and not notice anything.

They sit you down.

Show you the rubout scene from *St. Valentine's Day Massacre*.

If you don't see anything illegal going on, you're hired.

———

My favorite part of wrestling is when they bounce back and forth off the ropes

and crash in the middle like they're completely out of control.

A guy comes off the ropes,

"Oh no, my opponent is directly in my path.

There's nothing I can do.

I'm a prisoner of inertia."

They don't want to slam into each other, you see . . .

But the momentum is too great.

Cops/Posse

I think I could enjoy a career in law enforcement.

Seems like fun catching people doing stuff.

But I'm not really the right type of person because I would enjoy it TOO much.

I would catch somebody speeding and go,

"I got you, I got you, I got you. Eighty miles an hour, I got you so good . . . !"

That's obnoxious.

People like to catch people.

That's why in the Old West they had the posse.

Everybody wanted to be involved

You probably couldn't have the posse today because people don't have time.

And they have phone machines so they could screen their way out of it.

"Yeah, Bill, this is Jim . . . We're trying to get a posse together . . .

Bill? . . . Are you there? . . .

. . . Bill, c'mon, pick it up . . . I know you're there . . . Come on, one posse . . ."

———

Why do they still have to read that whole,

"You have the right to remain silent" speech to every criminal they arrest?

Is there anybody who doesn't know that by now?

Can't they just go,

"Freeze, you're under arrest. You ever seen *Baretta*?"

"Yeah."

"Good, get in the car."

Professional Football

Professional football.

To me the hardest part of being a professional football player

is on the one hand you're a millionaire.

On the other, they blow a whistle and you have to run around after a football.

To me, the whole idea of being a millionaire is,

somebody throws a football at me.

Maybe I catch it.

Maybe I don't.

I would think you get someone to hand you the football at that point.

"Here you go, sir, that's another touchdown for you.

Would you like a fresh squeezed orange juice before the next play?"

Time Save

We all try and save time.

All our little shortcuts.

But no matter how much time you save,

at the end of your life, there's no extra time saved up.

You'll be going,

"What do you mean I'm out of time?

I had a no-iron shirt,

Velcro sneakers,

clip-on tie:

Where is that time?"

It's not there.

Because when you waste time in life, they subtract it.

Like if you saw *all* the Rocky movies, they deduct that.

So, you've got to be careful.

You can take the Concorde to Europe,

but if they show *Porky's* on the plane,

you're right back where you started from.

Oscar Mayer

I try to eat healthy food.

It's really not that hard.

Some products are really very candid about their nutritional quality.

Certainly those Oscar Mayer cold cuts labeled simply "Luncheon Meat" fall into this category.

Here you have a product where it seems

even the manufacturer is not quite sure what the hell it is.

All they're telling you is,

"It's some kind of meat and you should eat it . . . around noon."

That's it.

I think they figure,

"You could never face it for breakfast.

No one would have the balls to serve it for dinner.

It's Luncheon Meat."

"We saw an animal.

We grabbed it.

Never got a real good look at him . . ."

Which is nothing compared to that other item,

Head Cheese.

Whooaaa . . .

I don't know what this is.

But the words "head" and "cheese" should never be that close together for any reason.

I'll try Head Meat before I go near this item.

Plants

I have such trouble with plants, they're so hard to keep alive.

Any little thing, you know you're supposed to play them music.

If I play one weak song.

That's it.

Suicide.

I come home, I find it hanging from a little macramé noose.

The pot kicked out from underneath.

Even left me a note, said, "I hate you and your albums."

Dead Pillow

The proof that we don't understand death is we give dead people a pillow.

Are they uncomfortable?

If you can't stretch out and get some solid rest at that point . . .

I don't think there are any bedding accessories that are going to make a difference.

And why do we have the guy all dressed up in a suit?

Is he sleeping, is he going to an important meeting?

Is he going to nap in a meeting?

We need to decide where we think these people are going.

Telephone Sales

One of the jobs I had starting out was

telephone lightbulb salesman.

For real.

First thing I learned was,

the world doesn't really need telephone lightbulb salesmen.

There's not a lot of people sitting home in the dark going,

"I can't hold out much longer.

If someone doesn't call pretty soon . . ."

Desk Family Pictures

Why do people who work in offices

have pictures of their family on their desk facing them?

Do they forget that they're married?

Do they say to themselves,

"All right. Five o'clock.

Time to hit the bars and pick up some hookers.

Hold it a second, look at this picture.

I've got a wife and three kids.

Oh my god, I better get home."

Sweepstakes Letter

I did get some very exciting news recently.

And I don't know if I should really even be talking about it,

because it's really not a definite thing yet . . .

. . . All right, well, I will tell you what I do know so far.

According to the information that I have,

in the envelope that I received,

it seems . . . that I may have already won some very valuable prizes.

Thank you, thank you very much.

Now remember, they're not saying anything definitely yet.

To be honest with you, I didn't even know I was in this thing.

But apparently I am among the top people at this point.

They're not saying I definitely won.

I may have.

I may have already lost.

You never get an envelope like that.

Just once I'd like to get a really hostile one.

"You have definitely lost.

Ha ha ha."

You turn it over, giant printing:

"NOT EVEN CLOSE."

Inside there is this whole letter of explanation.

"Even we cannot believe how badly you've done in this contest.

Never have we had such unanimous agreement that someone should NOT win.

You have the least luck of anyone we've ever seen.

Don't ever bother us again.

You make us physically ill."

Hallmark Greeting Cards

People are so confused about relationships these days.

You can tell just by the greeting cards.

They have a whole section of greeting cards now with no writing inside.

It's like Hallmark is saying,

"Hey, we don't know what to tell her.

You think of something, pal.

For 65¢ I don't want to get involved."

Date Job Interview

I like dating because I like tension.

There's dating going on in this room right now.

Feel that . . . ?

That's dating tension.

What is a date, really, but a job interview that lasts all night?

The difference is, not too many job interviews

is there a chance you'll end up naked at the end of it.

"Well, Jim, the boss really thinks you're the man for the job.

Why don't you strip down so you can meet some of the people you'll be working with . . ."

Movie Theaters

I was thinking about going to the movies tonight.

I just couldn't decide if I wanted to go to a "specially selected theater."

Or just a "theater near you."

How do these theaters know where I am?

If I move, do they move the theater?

Seems like a pretty expensive service.

Movie Candy

We're taking a pretty good beating on that candy, though, I'll tell you that.

You know the candy is going to be expensive when you see they display it in a glass case.

It's a jewelry case for candy.

This gives you some idea what they think it's worth.

"I'd like to see something in a Milk Dud, if I could."

He puts it on the fold-out black velvet display panel.

"Honey, what do you think?

That's a 2-carat Dud."

Personal Maintenance

Let's face it, the human body is like a condominium apartment.

The thing that keeps you from really enjoying it is the maintenance.

There's a tremendous amount of daily, weekly, monthly, and yearly work that has to be done.

From showering to open-heart surgery, we're always doing something to ourselves.

If your body was a used car, you wouldn't buy it.

You'd go,

"Nah, I've heard about these human being bodies.

This is one of those Earth models, right?

Yeah, a cousin of mine had one.

Too much work to keep them going.

The new ones are nice looking, though."

Deodorant Soap

Deodorant soap has always been kind of a mystery to me.

If you're covering your entire body, hands and face with deodorant, don't we have a larger problem?

If you smell this bad, maybe just call in sick?

"Listen, I can't come in today.

It's happening again.

I'll be at the zoo if you need me.

I think that's where I'll feel most comfortable."

The Last Soap Sliver

Well, I'm getting down to that last little sliver of soap in my shower.

I'm going to have to make a decision pretty soon.

Throw it out or try and mind-meld it to a new bar.

When does this add up to be a worthwhile activity?

One day you look around and you're hundreds of bars ahead of everybody else.

You're throwing Soap Parties.

Giving it away around the office.

"Hey, thanks. Where do you get it all?"

"I have my methods."

"Wow, that guy sure has a lot of soap."

"Yeah, he's quite a guy."

Men's Room

Then there's the Men's Room, which I hate.

I'm sure if I met a man outside that room,

I would find them to be a charming, delightful person.

But the Men's Room is a nauseating, disgusting place.

And every man in there is a sickening, revolting human slime.

You don't want to see, relate, or interact in any way

with any human in that room.

We won't even use our hands when we're in there.

Men operate everything with their feet as soon as they walk in.

We're like orangutans in the Men's Room.

Manipulating toilets, faucets, handles, everything.

They ought to put the ropes in there.

So we can just swing in . . .

Pee.

Swing out.

Facial Quality

I bought toilet paper the other day.

On the package I noticed it said, "Facial Quality."

I didn't care for the insinuation.

What's my *face* got to do with it?

When I buy facial tissue I don't look for "rectal quality."

When we were kids, we'd go,

"Got a match?"

"Yeah, my ass and your face."

That wasn't a compliment.

Cologne Set

For those of you in the back,

I am wearing cologne.

I don't know why.

Am I hoping, "Maybe people will think I really smell like this . . ."?

Someone gave me one of those gift sets that has cologne, aftershave, soap-on-a-rope.

I need soap-on-a-rope.

Lot of times I'm in the shower, I want to hang myself.

Why put these items together?

Because they rhyme?

I don't need shaving cream on a wooden beam.

This set even had underarm deodorant with the cologne smell.

Do you need cologne in there?

Once a woman's got her nose in your armpit, I think the seduction is pretty much over.

I think she likes you.

What are we, dogs?

Do you have to smell every square inch of a person before you make up your mind?

Even dogs just go by looks once in a while.

―――

When women put on their perfume they're very careful.

They always hit the inside of the wrist.

Women are convinced that this is the most action-packed area.

Why, ladies? What is happening there?

Is that in case you slap the guy?

He still finds you intriguing . . . ?

—CRACK!—

He turns back, ". . . Chanel."

In Sickness

The best time to be in a relationship is when you're sick.

And the best time to be sick is when you're in a relationship.

When I get married, I don't think I'll need all those different vows.

Just the sickness part.

That's the most important one to me. My whole wedding ceremony will be,

"Do you take this man in sickness?"

The rest of the time go out, have a ball, do whatever you want.

But the second I have a temperature, you better be there.

Have Kids

I'd like to have a family someday.

Although it's hard to imagine being the head of the household

when my life at this point consists mostly of wandering around my apartment, kicking underwear up in the air and trying to catch it.

A Giant On-Off Switch

Your car breaks down.

You get out of the car.

Walk around the front . . .

Open the hood . . .

And then do the big "Look In."

"Well, there it is . . .

That's the car.

Boy, I wish I knew what was going on in there."

We're hoping that we will see something that's so obvious.

So simple.

So easy to fix.

Even you can do it.

Like a giant On/Off switch turned "OFF."

"Okay . . . I think I can fix this."

It's That Guy

No matter whatever else you do in life, having a kid is the big step.

I think you get to a point where everybody you know has pretty much caught on to you.

You need to create a new person, someone that doesn't know anything about you.

You need a relationship with a person who's impressed that you know where the spoons are.

That's the level.

Where to urinate.

This is why you have kids.

They really look up to you in these areas.

Of course, the kid matures, becomes intelligent and leaves the house.

That is why people get pets.

Dogs stay stupid.

They never catch on to anything.

Every time you come home, he thinks it's amazing.

"You're back again!!

(sings)

It's that guy . . .

That guy is back . . .

With the ball and the food . . .

It's that guy . . .

—How did you know which house I was in?"

Parking Lots

In parking lots now, they have these "Compact Car Only" spots.

Isn't that discrimination against the size of your car?

If I want my ass hanging out of the back of my parking spot, that's my business.

There are people out there with real asses hanging out of their pants, nobody's stopping them.

Nobody goes,

"Hey, hold it, sir, those are compact jeans, you can't pull that in there."

The
Eighties

On May 6, 1981, I walked out, a bit stiffly, onto *The Tonight Show* starring Johnny Carson.

Six minutes later, as the audience continued applauding, I started back toward the curtain.

Over the applause, Johnny asked me to come back and "take a bow."

My four-year-old absurd dream had come true.

I was a comic.

I had moved to LA from New York a year earlier with my life savings of $2,000.

I slept on my friend George Wallace's couch at 733 West Knoll Drive, Apartment 129, in West Hollywood.

The first thing I did upon arriving was buy a used '74 Fiat 124 sedan, which was a very solid little car, for $2,000 and I was back to zero.

Comedians talked about getting on Johnny Carson like Dorothy talked about going home.

Could not shut up about it.

It was a high bar to clear.

You had to have killer stuff.

Fresh, original and, of course, completely clean.

And you could not do more than six minutes to show it all off.

In that moment, standing there by yourself,

getting laughs from a big studio crowd as it goes out live to a national network TV audience is like sliding down the face of the biggest wave you've ever surfed

You get back behind that curtain

and you want to collapse like a hundred-meter sprinter at the finish.

"That's everything I have," is the subtext of that set.

You know it.

Your friends know it.

Your family knows it.

And now everybody knows it.

———

So that was really the starting gun going off of my comedy life in the eighties.

I already knew that one good TV talk show set was not going to be nearly enough.

But I had long ago focused in on this being my only life interest anyway.

I had other life experiences of course, but they always felt very light and thin compared to my life in comedy.

It wasn't for many, many years that I even began to consider that there might be

other important things in the human experience besides doing stand-up and getting laughs.

Might be.

Still thinking about it.

I'll let you know.

Friendly Pilot Chit Chat

I think I've heard just about all the friendly little pilot chit chat

I need to hear for the rest of my life.

They always want to tell us how much pleasure it is having us on board.

The guy flies a plane every day.

How much pleasure is it?

"I don't know who's back there today but these people are fantastic."

And they always want us to,

"Sit back . . . relax . . . enjoy the flight."

Yeah. We're back. We're sitting.

This is as back as we can sit.

We don't want to relax.

We want to get there.

You ever wish you had your own little intercom at the seats so you could talk back to him?

"Yo, hey, Chuck . . .

It's Jerry. I'm back here in 23C.

Just want you to know we're all feeling really 'good to go' back here . . .

How about you just hit the gas and we bust out?"

Then for some reason he has to tell us all about what he's doing . . .

"Well, I'm going to take it up to about 20,000.

Then I'm going to make a left by Pittsburgh.

I'm going to make a right by Chicago.

Then, I'm going to bring it down to 15,000."

(crackle) "Yeah, Chuck. Jerry again . . .

We're all fine with all that.

Our feeling is why don't you just do whatever the hell you have to do?

Just end up where it says on the ticket, really.

That's our only focus, honestly."

Do I bother him with what I'm doing?

Knocking on the cockpit door,

"I'm having the peanuts now.

Yeah, that's what we're doing back here.

I thought I would keep YOU posted.

On what I'M doing.

I'm not going to have them all now.

I'm going to have a few.

I don't want to finish it because it's such a BIG BAG."

Keys to the Plane

The other day on a plane I thought,

"I wonder if there's keys to the plane?

Do they need keys to start the plane?"

Maybe that's what those delays on the ground are sometimes.

When you're just sitting there at the gate.

Maybe the pilot's up there in the cockpit going,

"Oh, I don't believe this . . . dammit . . . I did it again."

They tell you it's something mechanical, because they don't want to come on the P.A. system,

"Ladies and gentlemen, we're going to be delayed here on the ground for a little while.

I, uh . . . oh god, this is so embarrassing . . . I, I left the keys to the plane in my apartment.

They're in this big blue ashtray by the front door.

I'm really sorry. I'll run back and get them."

You see the technicians all running around underneath the plane.

You think they're servicing it,

but they're actually looking for one of those magnet Hide-A-Keys under the wing.

Stewardess Emergency Equipment Show

Then the stewardesses have to come out.

They have to do their little Emergency Equipment Show.

One of them reads it.

The other one acts it out.

(singing)

"Hey, we have seatbelts . . . oxygen masks.

(turns to the side, marching motion)

And things for you to use . . ."

———

They show you how to use a seatbelt.

In case you haven't been in a car since 1965.

"Oh, you lift up on the buckle . . . oooh!

I was trying to break the metal apart.

I thought that's how it works.

I was going to try and tear the fabric part of the belt.

(teeth gnawing on it)

I thought if I could just get it started . . ."

Then they always point out the emergency exits.

Always with that very vague point though, isn't it?

(pointing randomly)

Where the hell would these places be, would you say?

The plane's at a 90-degree angle.

Your hair is on fire.

(vague point)

You're looking for this.

You think you'll be alright?

She's thinking,

(pointing)

"I'm getting out—before you're getting out.

You're dead, you're dead, you're dead.

I'm gone."

They always have to close that first-class curtain, too.

They always give you that little look.

"Maybe if you had worked a little harder . . .

I wouldn't have to do this."

(swoosh shut)

Airport Cart People

I believe the closest thing we have to royalty in America

are the people that ride in those little carts through the airport.

They come out of nowhere.

"Beep, beep. Cart people, look out, cart people!"

We all scurry out of the way like worthless peasants.

"Ooh, it's cart people. I hope we didn't slow you down.

Wave to the cart people, Timmy.

They're the best people in the world."

If you're too fat, slow, and disoriented to get to your gate on time, you're not ready for air travel.

Airplane Bathroom

When I'm on an airplane I always go in the airplane bathroom.

Even if I don't have to go.

I just like that little room.

It's like your own little apartment on the plane, isn't it?

You go in, close the door, the light comes on after a second.

It's like a little surprise party.

I like a tiny world.

Tiny sink, tiny soap, tiny mirror.

And a little slot for used razor blades.

Who is shaving on the plane?

And shaving so much,

they're using up razor blades.

Is the Wolfman flying in there?

Who else could shave that much?

"Argh! . . . click, click (changes blades) . . . argh!"

———

I also love the sign,

"As a courtesy to the next passenger, please wipe off the counter with your towel."

Well, let me earn my wings every day.

Sorry I forgot to bring my toilet-bowl brush with me.

When did this Brotherhood of Passengers get started?

"Did they lose your luggage?

Here, take mine.

We're all passengers together.

By the way, was that bathroom clean enough for you?

I couldn't find the Comet or I would've had that crapper gleaming."

Airport Tuna Sandwich

Do the stores in the airport have any idea

what the prices are every place else in the world?

Or do they just feel they have their own little country out there,

and they can charge anything they want?

"You want a tuna sandwich? It's 28 dollars.

If you don't like it, go back to your own country."

I think the whole airport/airline complex is a huge scam just to sell the tuna sandwiches.

I think that profit is what's supporting the entire air-travel industry.

The planes could fly empty, they'd still make money.

The terminals, the airplanes, the parking, the gift shops.

It's all just to distract you, so you don't notice the beating you're taking on the tuna.

Airport X-Ray

I feel safe in airports, too.

And I think the main reason for that is the high-caliber individuals we have working at the X-ray security counters.

Here's a crack squad of savvy, motivated personnel.

The way you want to set up your airport security is

you want the short, heavyset woman at the front with the skin-tight uniform.

That's your first line of defense.

You want those pants so tight, the flap in front of the zipper has pulled itself open and you can

see the metal tangs of the zipper hanging on for dear life.

Then you put the bag on the conveyor belt.

Goes through the little luggage car wash.

Then you have that other genius down at the end looking in the little X-ray TV screen.

This Einstein has chosen to stand in front of X-rays 14 hours a day as his profession.

I've looked in that TV screen.

I cannot make out one object.

He's standing there,

"What is that, a hairdryer with a scope on it?

That looks okay . . . keep it moving.

Some sort of bowling ball candle?

Yeah, I've got no problem with that, we don't want to hold up the line."

———

What *would* they do if they ever came up against a real terrorist?

Start hitting him with those blue popcorn buckets?

"Hey, quit hijacking!"

They'd probably ask him to try going through the detector again *without* the uzi,

"This is probably what set it off."

Then give it back to him on the other side.

"No problem, it was probably your gun belt that set it off. Are those metal bullets?

Yeah. Sorry to hold you up. Was this your bomb? And the bazooka, rocket launcher?"

"Hey, that guy's got a ring of keys, somebody grab him."

Drugs at Customs

I went through customs recently.

The guy asks me,

"Any plants?"

"No."

"Any alcohol?"

"No."

Then he says,

"Any drugs?"

Is he catching people like this?

"Any drugs?"

"Bingo, you got me.

Slap the cuffs on.

I don't know how you did it.

I was not expecting that question."

Plane Crash

I don't know why people always have the same reaction when they hear about a plane crash.

"Really? Where?"

"Plane crash? What airline?"

As if it makes some difference . . .

Like you're going to go,

"Oh, that flight.

Oh, okay.

That I can understand."

Like there are some planes that are expected to crash.

You go up to the ticket agent,

"Excuse me, this flight generally goes down quite a bit, doesn't it?"

"Actually it does, yes.

We do have another flight but it tends to explode on takeoff.

Although, it is a snack flight."

Distance by Time

You can measure distance by time.

"How far away is that place?"

"About 20 minutes."

But it doesn't work the other way.

"When do you get off work?"

"Around 3 miles."

Hotels

I like hotels because I enjoy tiny soap.

I like to pretend it's normal soap and that my muscles are huge.

The other thing I wonder about in hotels is,

how do they get the Kleenex to come out of the bathroom walls?

Do they put those boxes in there when the building is built?

When they're all used up,

do they have to break down the wall,

put in a new box?

It's a lot of work for the flush-fit appearance.

And by the way, you can always tell when you're staying in a fine quality, luxury hotel . . .

When the television set is *welded* to a solid steel beam, *bolted* into the wall.

Do people come up to the desk?

(TV set under arm)

"I'd like to check out . . .

very quickly, please."

Hotel Fire

I love the fire map on the door of the hotel room.

I'm flattered that they think I have it together enough

to stand in a burning hotel room memorizing directions.

". . . Okay . . . left by the ice machine . . . past the elevators . . ."

Of course, you get halfway out of the hotel,

get lost, have to go back to the room,

check the map again.

And it always says,

"Don't panic."

The hotel's on fire.

I've got 10 minutes to live.

It's my option.

I've never panicked my whole life.

I would like to experience that one time if I'm going out anyway.

And if they save you, you have a perfect excuse.

"I heard they found you naked,

swinging from the shower curtain,

with the ice bucket on your head. What happened?"

"I panicked."

"That's completely understandable."

Hawaii License Plate

The other day I saw a car with a Hawaii license plate.

Then I went,

"Wait a minute, how did that get here?"

I went down to the beach, there were tracks coming out of the water.

Northeast Guy

Nice day today here.

Or not.

Who cares?

I don't even know.

I'm a Northeast guy.

I like whatever the weather.

Because that is the weather for the day that it is.

Here's your choice:

You're dead.

Or it's today.

Those are the options.

You either don't exist or, occasional drizzle.

Take your pick.

No interest in what it

Might be

Could be

Should be

Used to be.

When people mention weather, I cannot pretend to care.

I cannot keep the conversation going.

"Can you believe this weather?"

"Yes, I can."

"Do you think it's going to stay like this?"

"No—I don't."

Indoors stays the same. Go there.

People can't believe the weather, these are the same people who can't believe the time.

"Is it 3 o'clock already?

I can't believe it's 3 o'clock."

"Well, it is.

Every day at this time it's 3 o'clock."

Can't believe the time.

Can't believe the temperature.

Why don't you hang out in front of the bank sign all day?

Every time it changes you can go,

"Incredible. Another shocker.

Is anybody else seeing this?"

Cow's Leather

I have a leather jacket that got ruined because it got wet.

Suede jacket.

I was out in the rain.

Ruined.

Why?

Why does water ruin leather?

Aren't cows outside a lot of the time?

When it rains do they go up to the farm house,

"Hey, let us in, we're all wearing leather out here!"

"Is it suede?"

"Suede?

I am suede.

I've been living suede every day of my life!"

Public Speaking

I saw a study that said,

the number one fear of the average person is public speaking.

Number two is death.

Death is number two!

How in the world is that?

That means to most people,

if you have to go to a funeral,

you would rather be in the casket than doing the eulogy.

Neil Armstrong's Toothbrush

I was at the Air and Space Museum at the Smithsonian Institution.

They have all kinds of exhibits about the astronauts.

They show you the food they ate and everything.

They even had Neil Armstrong's toothbrush on display.

In a glass case.

Underneath it said,

"On loan from Neil Armstrong."

And I'm thinking,

"Neil—give them the brush."

I mean, they flew him to the moon.

No charge.

Get—another—brush.

So they asked him for his toothbrush and he says,

". . . I could lend it to you."

Is he coming in at night and using it?

Bathrobe, slippers, Colgate in his hand.

"I'm going to need the brush . . .

If everyone's done LOOKING at it . . ."

Monkey Astronauts

Monkeys have contributed a lot to society.

They were the first astronauts in the '60s.

Which I'm sure made perfect sense in the monkey brain.

"I see, so instead of the little bellhop uniform,

you want me to get into a rocket and orbit the Earth at super-sonic speed.

Yeah, I think that is the next logical step for me.

Because, I've been working with the Italian guy and the crank organ, and I feel ready to handle the maximum re-entry G-forces."

Get Candy

Your whole motivation in life when you're a kid is GET—CANDY.

It was like a mantra running through every second of every day.

"GET CANDY, GET CANDY, GET CANDY."

Friends, family, school.

These were just obstacles in the way of getting more candy.

You pretend you're talking to people, doing things.

But inside your head, candy is your only real goal.

Remember how they would tell us,

"If you're in a playground, and a stranger in a car offers you candy,

DON'T TAKE IT."

They had to drill that into us.

Because if they didn't, we had such candy, moron, idiot brains.

We would be like,

"This man has candy.

I'm going with him, I don't care what happens to me.

Get candy, get candy, get candy."

"Wait, no, don't. They'll kidnap you. They'll kill you."

"I don't care.

He has Oh, Henry!

I have to take that chance."

Halloween/Candy

So, the first time you even hear the word "Halloween" when you're a kid, you're like,

"What is this, what did you say?

What are you talking about . . . ?

They're giving out candy?

Who is giving out candy?

EVERYONE THAT WE KNOW IS JUST GIVING OUT CANDY??!!

When? Where? How?

Take me with you!

I've got to be a part of this!

What do you have to do?

(listens . . .)

I can wear that!

I'll wear whatever I have to wear.

I'll do whatever I have to do.

To get the candy from those fools who are so stupidly just giving it away."

First couple of years, I went as a ghost, hobo, the worst.

Then finally, I was able to convince my parents to get me the Superman Halloween costume

from the store. I was certain this was going to be my greatest trick-or-treating year.

Cardboard box, cellophane top, mask included in the set.

And the wonderful innocence and stupidity of the time.

On the side of the box there was a warning that for real said:

"Do not attempt to fly."

Really was.

Because kids were putting the costume on and going off their roofs.

I love the idea of the kid who is stupid enough to think he's Superman, because of the ridiculous costume.

But smart enough to check the box before he jumps off a building.

"Let me just double-check here . . . if it says anything about me actually being Superman.

Oh hold on, hold on, wait a second . . . it says here . . ."

The rubber band on that mask was made to last about half a second.

The thinnest gray rubber in the world.

Cheap little staple they attach it with.

You go to your first house, "Trick or (snap) . . . It broke."

You don't even get to "treat."

"Wait, I got to fix it. Wait up for me."

Kids don't want other kids to wait.

They want them to "wait up."

Because when you're little, your life is up, the future is up, everything you want is up.

"Wait up.

Hold up.

Shut up.

Mom, I'll clean up.

Just let me stay UP."

For parents everything is down.

"Calm down.

Slow down.

Come down here.

Sit down.

Put that down.

You are GROUNDED."

So, I get the Superman Halloween costume.

First of all, it's not exactly the super-fit that you have seen in movies and on television.

It's more like Superman's pajamas.

Everything's all loose and flowy.

Flimsy little ribbon string in the back to hold it all together.

Plus, my mother makes me wear my winter coat over the costume anyway.

I don't recall Superman wearing a jacket.

Not like I had.

Cheap corduroy, phony fur.

"Boy, I'm Superman but it is a little chilly out today.

I'm glad I've got this cheap little ten-year-old-kid's jacket."

So I'm going out, I'm trick-or-treating.

But the mask's rubber band keeps breaking.

I keep re-tying it.

It keeps getting shorter.

It's getting tighter and tighter on my face.

It starts slicing into your eyeballs.

You're trying to breathe through that little hole.

It gets all sweaty in there.

"I can't see, I can't breathe, but we've got to keep going, we've got to get the candy!"

Half an hour into it, you just take that mask and just throw it . . .

"Aah, the hell with it!"

Bing-bong . . .

"Yeah, it's me. Just give me the candy.

Yeah, yeah . . . I'm Superman.

Look at the red pant legs, what do you care?"

Last couple years, getting too old for it.

Just going through the motions.

You start to realize you're putting in a lot of time.

It's a lot of walking.

By the end of that night you're losing patience.

You ring the doorbell,

"Come on, lady, let's go."

Halloween. Doorbells. Candy.

Let's pick it up, in there . . .

Same questions over and over.

"And what are you supposed to be?"

"I'm supposed to be done by now, could we move it along with the Three Musketeers, please?

I've got 12 houses to hit on this block, sweetheart.

I'm tired.

I got eggs, water balloons to throw.

I'm trying to get off my feet by 11.

Can we pick up the pace?

You hit the bag.

We hit the road.

That's how it works."

Sometimes you get those little white paper bags twisted on top.

No official Halloween markings on it?

You know that's going to be some crap candy.

"What is this, the orange marshmallow shaped like a big peanut?

Do me a favor, you keep that one.

(Throws it back)

We've got all the doorstops we need already.

We're going for name candy only this year."

Braces Glasses

I had glasses at 10, braces at 12.

When you're thinking about talking to a girl for the very first time in your life,

you want as much corrective apparatus on your head as you can possibly get.

I said to my parents,

"Let's not stop now, how about a hearing aid, orthopedic shoes?

I want to look like a human science project.

Sparks flying out from behind my head.

This is my image.

Let's go with it."

Bugs Going?

I have always wondered,

where are bugs going?

Every bug you see is on his way somewhere else.

Bugs never seem to stop and go,

"Well, here I am."

And if you put your hand down in front of him, no problem.

They pick a completely different destination.

But I guess if you were walking along,

and someone dropped a 200-foot wall in front of you,

you'd go,

"I think I'll go elsewhere.

There's walls falling out of the sky around here.

I don't need that."

Sometimes I would flick a bug like, 20 feet.

Which is the farthest from home he's ever been.

He has to hitchhike to get back.

He's holding a little sign,

"20 feet."

Did Comets Kill the Dinosaurs?

Magazines are another medium I love.

Because like TV, 95% of it is simply based on,

"How the hell are we going to fill all this blank space?"

The cover of *Time* magazine this week was,

"Did Comets Kill the Dinosaurs?"

Really?

Here's a hot topic—who's got time for this?

"Hey, what happened to the dinosaurs? Weren't they just here?"

Maybe comets did kill the dinosaurs.

Maybe they tripped and fell.

What's the difference?

We'll never know.

We couldn't solve the Kennedy assassination and we had film on that.

Good luck with the stegosaurus.

"Round up all these reptiles for questioning, Bill.

I want to talk with that little salamander over there.

I think he knows something.

Don't stick your tongue out at me, young man.

I'll nail your slimy little butt to the wall."

Fun for the Whole Family

At the post office they have posters,

"Collect stamps, it's fun."

Really?

At what point in stamp collecting do you feel the fun is really kicking in?

You get the stamp.

Bring it home.

Put it in a drawer.

Come back a year later,

"Hey . . . still got it.

That stamp is COLLECTED."

I guess if you ever get bored of the stamps,

you can turn them over, you've got a glue collection.

They always say,

"Fun for the Whole Family."

Nothing is fun for the whole family.

There's no massage parlors with ice cream and free jewelry.

No racetrack sells fur coats and Silly Putty.

Ancient Cultures

I like documentaries.

But not every ancient culture is fascinating.

I think in some cases, *extinction* may have been their luckiest break.

Like when they tell you about some ancient people

that lived right on the rim of an active volcano.

How much can we learn from people that stood around during an eruption going,

"Boy, it is hot today.

Did the weatherman say 'lava'?

I heard 'chance of molten' by the weekend."

Air Inside Outside

To me, the whole city of Los Angeles is a mall.

It's temperature controlled, plenty of parking.

You don't really like it but you can get whatever you need while you're there.

The thing about LA that kind of threw me was the smog alerts.

They will sometimes actually recommend that people stay indoors during the smog alert.

Wouldn't you assume that the air in the house pretty much comes from the air in the city where the house is?

Do they think we live in a jar with a couple of holes punched in the top?

Do parents in LA say to their children,

"All right, kids! I want all of you in the house to get some fresh air!

Come on, it's summer vacation.

Indoors!"

New Mexico

To me, the ballsiest name for a state would have to be New Mexico.

I mean, you're *right next* to Mexico.

"Well, we're going to be *New* Mexico."

What if your name is Bob Johnson, somebody moves next door, rings your bell and says,

"Hi. I've decided I'm going to be New Bob Johnson."

What's Mexico supposed to say?

"Well then, we'll be Mexico Classic."

Magician

I don't think anything competes with a magic act for humiliating entertainment.

What is the point of the magician?

He comes on.

He fools you.

You feel stupid.

Show's over.

You never know what actually happened.

It's never explained.

And that's kind of the attitude the magician seems to have as he's performing.

He's like,

"Here's a quarter.

Now, it's gone.

You're a jerk."

Sometimes they ask you to blow on it to make you feel even more pathetic.

I also love that condescending little pretend look of surprise they do when the trick works.

Like,

"Oh. I didn't know that was going to happen myself.

I am also quite entertained by my own wizardry."

Bullet Catch

You know there is an actual guy that can catch a bullet between his teeth?

There is.

I saw him on *That's Incredible!*

And it was.

I remember seeing it and then actually saying, "That's incredible."

Although I can't remember his name.

Which is terrible.

Because if he knew that I had seen him do that and then couldn't remember his name,

wouldn't he feel like,

"What the hell do I have to do to really impress people?

Catch a cannonball in the eye?"

I'd like to know what he was doing before he got into catching bullets.

I mean, how bad could a job be?

"You know, to tell you the truth, I'd rather catch bullets in my teeth than do this."

How do you even know that you would be good at this?

Do they throw it at you a few times first? Really hard.

Put it in the gun and go,

"Okay, Bill . . . this one's going to be coming a little bit faster now.

We're going to pick up the pace quite a bit . . ."

If you're a burglar, this is definitely a house you don't want to break into.

Surprise him in the bedroom,

(spits it out)

"I think you got the wrong house, pal.

What is that, a .22?

I hate those."

McDonald's Sign

So, what's the McDonald's sign up to now, 89 billion?

89 billion hamburgers.

It's such an outrageous number.

"89 billion? Wow. Okay. I'll have one."

I really want to someday meet the CEO of McDonald's. Just so I can say to him,

"Look, we all GET IT, okay?

You've sold A LOT of hamburgers.

A hundred million, zillion, cotillion, whatever the hell it is . . ."

Just put up a sign,

"McDonald's—we're doing very well."

We don't need to hear about every god damn one of them.

———

What is their ultimate goal?

To have cows just surrendering voluntarily?

Coming up to their door and going,

"We give up.

We'd like to turn ourselves in.

We see the sign.

We realize we have very little chance out there . . .

. . . I'd like to be a Happy Meal if that's at all possible . . ."

My Doctor Recommendation

People love to recommend their doctor to you.

I don't know what they get out of it,

but they really push them on you.

"Is he good?"

"Oh my god, he's the best. The absolute best."

There can't be this many "bests."

Someone's graduating at the bottom of these classes.

Where are these doctors?

Is someone, somewhere, saying to their friend,

"You should see my doctor, he's the worst.

Whatever you've got, it'll be worse after you see him.

The man's an absolute butcher."

And whenever a friend refers a doctor they say,

"Make sure you tell him that you know me."

Why? What's the difference?

He's a doctor.

"Oh, you know Bob?

Ohh, okay . . . I'll make sure you get the real medicine.

Everybody else I'm giving Tic Tacs."

Pharmacist Two Feet Up

And why does the pharmacist always have to be

two and a half feet higher than everybody else?

Brain surgeons.

Airline pilots.

We're all on the same floor level.

But not this guy.

Why?

"Spread out, everybody.

Give me some room.

I'm working with pills up here.

I'm taking them from this big bottle.

And I'm going to put them in a little bottle.

Then I've got to type some words on a really tiny piece of
paper.

That's my whole job.

Pills and tiny typing.

So, that's why I can't be down on the floor with you people.

You have no idea what it's like.

Four . . . five . . . six . . . hold it.

Dammit—

I think I lost count.

. . . you see?

It's hard.

That's why I have to be two and a half feet up!"

"Yes, I'd like to get this prescription filled, please."

"All right.

But you wait down there.

No one comes up here but me."

Supermarket Impulse Buy

When I was a kid I hated the supermarket.

You're with your mom.

Anything you want you have to beg for it like a trained poodle.

"Mom, please, these are different.

They have the chocolate on the inside."

So degrading.

Now, I get whatever I want in the supermarket.

The whole cart is filled with things that I want.

And if I decide I don't want something,

I put it back wherever I am in the supermarket.

There's no rules in the supermarket.

It's us against them.

They invented impulse buying.

We invented *impulse NOT buying*.

I don't care if the store manager is looking right at me.

"Yeah, those are my peaches on top of the Pennzoil. What about it?

I can't straighten out your whole inventory.

I'm busy here reading magazines I'm not going to buy either."

Supermarket Rubber Dividers

I also like those little rubber dividers they give you at the checkout.

Because you want your items,

and you want a little property there too.

Set up your rubber fence.

You don't want other people's items fraternizing with your items, do you?

There are two ways to use the rubber divider.

Sometimes you can put it down on the conveyor belt as most people do, or I just hold it in my hand,

(pointing with it)

"Hey, your potato chips are kind of creeping up on my box of donuts there, pal.

You want to back it off a bit?

Little cozy there, don't you think?

(hits him on the head)

Hey—*TOK*.

You listening to me?"

You need a little police action on these checkout lines, sometimes.

"Excuse me—*TOK*

13 items, buddy boy, you're over.

Count them up, read the sign, hit the road.

—*TOK*

I said move it."

Milk After the Day

You ever just stare at the milk in the supermarket wondering,

"Do we have milk?

Do we need milk?"

Even right now, I'm trying to think if I have enough milk and I really have no idea.

Because sometimes you think you have milk and you don't have milk.

You have the bowl set up, the cereal, the spoon, the napkin, the TV, the newspaper.

You go to pick up the milk, and you smash it into the roof of the refrigerator.

"Oh noo . . . too . . . light . . ."

Your muscles can't adjust to something that light.

No matter how little you work out—you're too strong.

And no, I don't throw it out.

I put it back in the refrigerator.

In case I get an urge for a sixteenth of an oatmeal cookie.

I might need an eyedropper of milk for it.

You have weird breakfasts when you're out of milk.

Three Kraft Singles and some tap water.

———

Or sometimes you think you need milk.

So you get milk.

But it turns out you had milk.

And now you've got way too much milk.

That's not good either.

Now, it's a race against the clock with the expiration date.

Now, you're eating giant punch bowls of cereal.

Three meals a day.

You're washing your face with milk.

Bringing cats in from all over the neighborhood.

"Hurry up and drink it!

Come on, it's almost time!

(one cat wanders away, it gets picked up)

Get back over here . . ."

How do they know that that is the definite exact day?

They don't say "around" that day.

They brand it right into the side of the carton.

"Sssssssss . . ."

"That's your god damn day right there!

Don't screw with us.

We know which day is the day."

You ever have milk the day after the day?

Scares the hell out of you, doesn't it?

The spoon is trembling as it comes out of the bowl.

"It's after the day."

"Did you smell it?"

"I smelled it.

You smell it.

What's it supposed to smell like?

I don't know what I'm smelling for.

It smelled like milk.

I don't know what the hell I'm doing here."

I don't know how they can be so sure.

Do the cows tip them off when they're milking them . . . ?

(slow turn of the head backwards)

". . . July . . . 3rd . . ."

Milk Monitor

No matter how much money I ever had, I'd never want a butler or a maid.

But I would pay to have a Milk Monitor.

Just a guy to stand by the refrigerator in an all-white suit, white shoes, white cap.

24 hours a day.

Then as I walk out the door he goes,

"You're okay for tomorrow."

I would pay for that.

Coffee World

Two things I've noticed:

There's a lot of jobs in the world.

And there's a lot of coffee.

Every building I've ever been in has coffee.

Every door I've ever opened in my life,

somebody on the other side of it went,

"Would you like a cup of coffee?"

"Can we get you some coffee?"

"How about coffee?"

"Fresh coffee?"

"Had coffee?"

"Need coffee?"

"More coffee?"

You can lift up a manhole cover,

(looking up)

"We just made a fresh pot, would you like some?

Decaf?

Next sewer."

People have coffee at home, coffee at work.

A mug on the dashboard of the car in case they can't make it.

Maybe we should have scuba tanks of coffee on our backs so we can just breathe it?

We used to have coffee breaks.

Now, it's all coffee.

No break.

There's Coffee Trucks.

Trucks of coffee driving around.

Just looking for people that want coffee.

To make sure everyone has coffee.

"Please stay where you are.

We have trucks in your area.

They will find you."

Only coffee has trucks like this.

There's no Broccoli Trucks.

"Beep, beep."

"Broccoli truck!"

Nobody comes out . . .

Mr. Coffee

I went to buy a coffee machine the other day.

I like coffee.

But these coffee machines never let you forget how much you need coffee.

I saw one machine,

BREWMASTER.

You wake up in the morning,

"Yes . . . BREWMASTER . . . I—will—make—a—full—pot—today."

MR. COFFEE.

I'm not even on a first-name basis with this one.

"Think I'll have a cup of coffee."

"Hey, that's 'MR.' Coffee to you, pal."

Post Office Annoyed

Why is it as soon as I walk in the post office,

I'm immediately annoyed?

I could be feeling good, having a good day.

As soon as I'm in that door, I'm just . . .

"Oh well, I guess all these people here are ahead of me . . .

Fine.

I'll just wait, then . . .

I will wait.

Because they got here a little bit before I did.

That's—just—great."

You know how you yell at people sometimes inside your head?

It's a good technique.

Keeps the world from being just an endless river of murder and bloodshed.

The post office is great for that.

All the people working behind the counter,

"Yeah, take a little bit longer giving that guy his change . . .

Oh terrific, now go in the back for 20 minutes and look for nothing in particular.

Great.

Wonderful.

I don't care.

I have no life and nothing else to do.

I'd like to stay on this line for the rest of the year if I can."

———

On the outside, you're just standing there holding your package.

Very placid expression . . .

On the inside, screaming at the top of your lungs,

(COME ON!!! MOVE UP!!! THERE'S A GAP IN FRONT OF YOU!!)

Everybody in front of you that gets to the counter at the post office

has some sort of problem with their package.

"I'm not sure about this knot I made here."

"I forgot to brush my teeth before I licked the stamp, do you think that'll affect the glue?"

Once, I gave the guy the package, he puts it on a table behind him.

Then I ask him,

"When do you think it'll get there?"

He turned around, looked at the package.

Then turned back to me and said,

"A few days."

What was he looking at?

Like he was going to ask the package,

"When do you plan on leaving?"

Why doesn't he just tell the truth?

"Look, I don't know. Nobody knows.

You think if we had any idea what we were doing here FedEx and UPS would be so huge?"

Watching postal employees work is like watching a lava lamp, isn't it?

They're just floating and oozing around back there.

I think there's a big lightbulb in the back.

That heats them up so they kind of float up to the front.

Sell a few books of stamps, then they cool and slowly drift into the back again.

That's how the postal system works.

Post Office Wanted Posters

Why are there Wanted posters at the post office?

You're there.

You've got your package.

You're trying to mail something.

This guy's wanted in 12 states.

All right . . . Now what?

I check the guy standing in line behind me.

If it's not him, that's pretty much all I can do.

What, are we supposed to rip one off the wall, go up to the counter,

"Yeah, give me a book of stamps and a search warrant.

I'm going after this guy.

I've had it up to here with his activities."

Why don't they hold on to this guy when they're taking his picture?

THE GUY IS THERE WITH YOU.

Come out from behind the camera, and GRAB him.

"No, we don't do that.

We take their picture.

We let them go.

That's the way we've always done it.

That's how we get the front and side shot.

The front is his face.

The side is him leaving."

Why don't they put the pictures of the criminals on the postage stamps?

Let the postman look for him.

He's out there walking around all day.

He's got the uniform on.

Can't he do something?

"We got a letter for you, Mr. Johnso—

... WAIT A MINUTE ... !"

Newspapers Perfect Fit

What amazes me about the newspaper is that somehow,

every day,

no matter what goes on in the world,

it exactly fits the number of pages they're using in the paper that day.

How does that always work out?

They never have big blank spots where nothing happened.

Never have to cram things in the margins

because there's too much occurring.

It's a perfect fit, every time.

They must stand around after each edition and go,

"I can't believe we just made it again.

Hurry up and get the paper out before there's any more stories.

If one more thing took place, we'd be screwed.

We'd have to put it in the crossword puzzle."

Execution Style

On the news they'll say that someone was murdered "Execution style."

What are the other styles?

Ranch?

Thousand Island?

Homestyle?

How would you kill someone homestyle?

Just pull the belt on their bathrobe tighter and tighter?

"There's only one thing that can leave a mark like that on a body.

Terry cloth.

This man was murdered homestyle."

Earthquake

I read a report about an earthquake where local officials trying to explain the damage said,

"The earthquake wasn't that bad.

It's just that the buildings weren't designed to withstand earthquakes."

Would you accept an explanation like that in a courtroom?

"Your Honor, my client didn't murder this man.

His body simply wasn't designed to withstand bullets."

The Button

So, they have this special military person that's with the
President all the time.

He's got The Button.

This guy's always there.

I think, wouldn't it be better to give the button to some guy

who's almost impossible to get ahold of?

"Did you tell him to push the button?"

"I can't find him.

I just left a message on his machine.

I told him, when he comes in

to make sure and blow up the entire world."

Campaign '88

I bet a lot of Americans are thinking the same thing about it.

In the back of your mind you're like,

"I'm sure once the actual election rolls around, there'll be other
choices.

Once the word gets out that they're hiring Presidents,

there'll probably be lots of new people coming in.

I'm sure these are just placeholders for now, probably."

Just the fact that someone thinks they should be the President

is proof that they're quite mentally off.

What kind of person is this?

That sits around,

"Let's see, who should be the most powerful person in government?

Commander in Chief of the Armed Forces?

Leader of the Free World?

You know, I've got to say . . . that sounds like me.

It sounds like something I would be good at.

I really strike myself as the best person there could possibly be for that kind of job."

No, you're not.

You're sick and deranged.

Who could be friends with this person?

You're at a ballgame,

"You know, I was thinking about being the most powerful person in the world."

You go,

"Uh-huh . . .

I was thinking about getting a hot dog."

Moose Air Lift

Did anyone see the moose air lift report?

I saw it on CNN.

I like to just leave it on in the background.

It's like News-Zak.

Background news.

So apparently there was some sort of moose problem.

And they had to move these mooses by helicopter.

One by one.

They'd put one in a harness.

And then they moved him, hanging from cables underneath the helicopter.

Here is an animal that's been on the ground for thousands of years as a species.

Suddenly he's hundreds of feet in the air.

And the look on his face was so funny.

He was looking around like,

"Well, I guess I can fly now . . .

I must have eaten some kind of a weird berry or something.

I'm Super Moose.

I must devote the rest of my life to fighting moose crime."

He tries changing directions by swinging his legs.

Nothing happens.

"I'm sorry, I don't know how to work this thing . . .

I just got these powers today."

Foam Balls

News people are getting more aggressive each year.

You can tell, even the foam balls on their microphones are getting bigger.

That's probably how news people talk about each other.

"Boy, how about the foam balls on that guy?

He really got his question in there."

I don't even know what those foam balls are for.

I think it's so they can bop people over the head and get their attention without hurting them.

"Hey, (*bop*) I asked you a question.

Excuse me, (*bop*) Senator.

(*bop*) Sir.

I was just wondering (*bop*) over here.

If you could just tell us (*bop*) . . . *what we want to know* . . ."

Stand by Me

I saw that movie *Stand by Me*.

Good movie.

But I don't remember having friends like that when I was 12 years old.

Where they put their hand on your shoulder,

"You know god has given you a special talent."

I remember a kid would put his hand on my shoulder

so he could push me off the sidewalk into the bushes.

"You know, god has given you a face for the bushes."

Star Trek

I keep my apartment neat.

My idea of the perfect living room would be the bridge of the starship *Enterprise*.

Big chair.

Wide screen.

Remote control.

Star Trek was such a perfect male fantasy.

Hurtling through space.

In your living room.

Watching TV.

That's why all the aliens were always dropping in.

Because Kirk was the only one that had the big screen.

"Klingon boxing?

Awesome.

Let's watch at yours."

Talk Show Host

How come talk show hosts never have any idea how much time they have?

They're always looking off camera . . .

"Do we have time for this?

How are we doing on time?

Are we out of time?"

IT'S YOUR OWN SHOW.

Why do you know nothing about how it works?

You never see Magnum, PI, go,

"Should I strangle this guy or are we going to take a break here?

I tell you what, I'll bonk him in the head,

we'll take a quick break,

when we come back, I'll drive in the car real fast.

Stay with us."

TV Flip

I love TV.

Need TV.

Watch TV.

TV. TV. TV.

I don't like the shows.

Just like TV.

Like flipping.

"Rerun . . .

Don't want that . . .

Can't believe that's on the air . . .

He's so stupid . . .

She's so stupid.

They're so stupid.

Everything is stupid . . ."

People come in,

"What are you watching?"

"TV . . ."

You go around once, you know there's nothing on.

But you make that second lap.

That's the sad one.

That's when you find out how flexible your entertainment standards really are.

"Hmm . . . maybe I judged that *Love Connection* a little too hastily . . ."

Men, of course, flip around much more than women.

Men are not interested in what's on TV.

Men are only interested in what else is on TV.

"Keep going . . .

Keep flipping . . .

Keep changing . . ."

"Hey, your whole family is on *60 Minutes*."

"Don't care . . ."

"That was a documentary about your life."

"Not interested . . ."

Keep going,

keep going.

We don't know what we want.

We only know that we don't want what we have.

Women want to see what the show is before they change the channel.

"Hang on a second. Let's see what this is . . .

Maybe we can nurture it, work with it, help it grow into something."

Because women nest and men hunt.

That's why we watch TV differently.

TV Sleep

You ever get to that point of watching TV where you're so out of it . . .

So beat.

So wasted.

Your eyes are closed,

your brain is unconscious,

and yet you're still somehow searching for entertainment?

Now, am I so stupid that I think I'm awake?

Or am I so bored,

I don't care that I don't even know what I'm not watching?

It doesn't matter.

The finger that hits the button on the remote control

is the last part of the human body to fall asleep.

Probably the last part to die too.

I bet I'll be six feet under.

And the finger will be going like,

"Okay, I'm dead . . .

Let's see what else is on."

They say your life flashes in front of your eyes.

I'll be going,

"What is this?

My life?

I've seen this . . . that's a rerun.

I'm not watching that again."

We Have Soda

The basic problem with TV

is everybody you see on TV

is doing something better than what you're doing.

Nobody on TV is just watching TV.

You never see anybody on TV half conscious,

sliding off the sofa

with potato chip crumbs on their shirt.

Some people on TV are having a little too much fun.

The soda commercial people.

Jumping, laughing, hugging.

Where does all this enthusiasm come from?

"We have soda! We have soda! We have soda!"

Have you ever been sitting there

drinking the exact same product they're advertising on TV at that moment?

They're spiking volleyballs,

Jet Skiing,

girls in bikinis driving Jeeps into the surf,

"Sodaaaa!"

I look at it, I think,

"Maybe I'm putting too much ice in mine . . ."

Movie Plot

I always get confused in any international, adventure, intrigue type movie.

I'm the guy you see after the movie, in the parking lot with his friends going,

"Oh, you mean that was the same guy from the beginning?

Oooohhh . . .

That's why after they stole the money he had the fake nose and the beard and then he didn't,

oooohhh . . ."

"Did you enjoy the movie?"

"Yes. I'm enjoying it here in the parking lot, but in there I had no idea what was going on."

Nobody will explain anything to you in a movie theater once you get confused.

(whispering)

"What is happening now?"

"Ssshhhh. Nothing."

"Nothing? This is all nothing? Then why did they film it?

I don't understand why they killed that guy.

I thought he was with them.

Wasn't he with them?

Why would they kill him if he was with them?"

"They—had—to."

"Oh, so he wasn't really with them . . .

I like that actor. He was the only guy I liked."

"Would you just watch the movie?"

"I am watching. I don't understand anything."

"You—know—as—much—as—I—do."

"I—KNOW—NOTHING.

Is this a space movie?

Is it a western?

Totally lost.

I hate this movie.

. . . I hate you too."

———

Why can't they have subtitles for the plot?

"Closed-captioned for the movie impaired."

I would go to these movies.

Little lines pop up,

"Don't worry about this guy. He's only in this one scene."

"Here's the name of the other movie you can't remember that you've seen this person in."

"This is too hard to explain. They'll tell you in the parking lot."

———

The one movie ad I don't get is,

"If you see only one movie this year . . ."

If you see only one movie this year, why go at all?

You obviously don't like going to the movies.

And going once a year is ridiculous pressure to put on a movie.

You're sitting there,

"All right, this is it for the next 51 weekends. Better be good."

Armrest Battle

Another reason I go to the movies is for the marathon 2-hour Battle of the Armrest with the

complete stranger sitting next to me.

You walk out, your friend asks, "Did you like the movie?"

"Forget the movie. Did you see how I had the armrest for the whole last hour?!

He went for popcorn, I moved right in.

Forget the movie. This is real life."

Movie Employee Age Gap

There definitely seems to be an age gap in the hiring policy at most movie theaters.

They never hire anyone over 15 or under 80.

So, the girl that sells the tickets, she's 10.

Then there's the guy that rips it, he's 102.

So, what happened in the middle there?

They couldn't find anybody?

It's like they want to show you how life comes full circle.

When you're 15, you're selling the tickets, then you leave.

You go out, you have a family, kids, marriage, career, grandchildren.

Eighty years later, you're back in the same theater, three feet away, ripping tickets.

Eighty years to move three feet.

Movie—TV

They think we don't notice them making these little changes on us, but we do.

Like the TV commercials mixed in with the legitimate previews.

It's like we're POWs strapped into theater seats, and they just do whatever they want to us.

It's a *movie* theater.

The whole reason you go there is for NOT TV.

You have to park, you have to walk, you have to pay.

I'll do it.

That's how bad I want NOT TV.

Then you get there.

Soda commercial. Jeans commercial.

I have that at home!

It's like going to a restaurant and the waiter says,

"The only thing we have on the menu is exactly what's in your refrigerator right now."

"Great.

I'll have the Cheez-Its, baking soda and some olive jar water."

Batman Crooks

My car was broken into.

Stole the tape deck.

I don't know who it was.

I assume it was crooks.

Called the police.

They were of course . . . shocked.

Everyone says you're supposed to report these things to the police.

It felt kind of silly.

There's nothing that can be done about it.

It's not like *Batman*, where there's four crooks in the city

and everybody pretty much knows who they are.

Very few crooks even go to the trouble to come up with a theme for their careers anymore.

It makes them a lot tougher to spot.

"They stole a CD player out of your car?

It could be the Penguin.

I think we'll be able to round him up.

He's dressed like a penguin."

Crook Head Protect

When the cops catch a crook

they hit him with the nightstick.

Get him in a chokehold.

Cuff him behind his back.

But then when they put him in the back of a police car,

they always keep their hand on the top of his head.

"You don't want to hit your head on the edge of the door, there.

That *really* hurts."

Crook Life

I do wonder about the crook life.

Like . . .

If you're a crook, how does it feel when you have to pay for something?

Terrible, I would think . . .

He throws a candy bar on the counter,

"I could've stolen that . . .

Today's my day off."

What can two crooks do for fun?

Go bowling?

Who's going to keep score?

Birthday party?

He gives you a present.

You can't show it to anyone, it might have been theirs.

Crook Reputation

I have not been to jail.

But I think about jail.

I don't know why.

I think about how I would fix up my cell.

How many push-ups I would do.

Because I live alone anyway, it's kind of the same.

I'm in solitary.

Why are these captured hijackers, criminals and mass murderers

always hiding their faces when they're being taken in?

They got the hoodie up.

The jacket over the head.

What is this man's reputation that he needs to worry about being recognized?

Is he speed dating?

Is he this close to getting that big corner-office promotion?

Afraid the boss is going to see him on TV?

"Wait a minute . . .

Isn't that Johnson from Sales?

Why, he's skyjacked an EgyptAir 747.

And he's started throwing bodies out onto the tarmac one by one.

I don't know if that's the kind of person we want heading up that new branch office."

Chalk Outline Guy

Of the many different jobs there are in police work

it seems to me that Chalk Outline Guy is definitely one of the better ones.

It's not too dangerous, the criminals are long gone.

I don't know who these guys are.

Maybe they're people who wanted to be sketch artists but couldn't draw too well.

"Uh, listen, Johnson, forget the sketches . . .

Do you think if we left the dead body right there on the sidewalk,

you could manage to trace around it? Could you at least do that?"

I don't even know how that helps them solve the crime.

They look at the thing on the ground,

"Oh, his arm was over his head when he hit the pavement.

That means the killer must have been . . . Jim."

Florida Law

My parents have lived on Long Island most of their lives.

They're in the process of moving down to Florida now.

They don't want to move to Florida.

But they're in their 60s and that's the law.

After a while they just come and get you.

Florida has Leisure Police.

It's a golf cart with a siren on top.

"Okay folks, get in the back . . .

Dad,

white pants, white belt, white shoes.

Let's go. You're done.

Drop the snow shovel right there.

I said drop it!"

They like to live in those minimum-security prisons down there.

That's where they put all the old people.

Why such heavy security?

You pull up to the guard gate booth, the big arm thing comes down in front of your car.

Who is stealing the old people?

What are they worth?

"I got a granny. Let's go . . . !"

Old People Drive

I just can't drive around there.

Old people drive slow, they sit low.

That's their motto.

The state flag of Florida should be just a steering wheel with a hat and two knuckles on it.

And the left turn signal on from when they left the house that morning.

That's a legal turn in Florida, by the way.

It's called an Eventual Left.

You can signal this week,

then turn any following year of your life.

What is the age when old people decide that when they back out of a driveway,

they're not looking anymore?

You know how they do that?

They just go,

(Looking forward. Puts the car in reverse.)

"Well, I'm old and I'm coming back.

I survived.

Let's see if you can."

Parent Ducklings

I definitely feel like I've grown up when I go shopping with my parents now.

The roles have begun to reverse.

Suddenly, I'm in *charge* and they're completely disorganized, going all over the store.

They're like little ducklings just wandering everywhere.

My father's,

"Quack. Quack, quack . . ."

"Mom, we lost Dad . . .

He's 3 stores down.

You want to catch up or should I go get him?"

My mother's,

"Quack, quack."

"Dad, we lost Mom.

She's going off in the other direction.

I'll try and get her, you wait here.

Please just tell me what is happening?"

You try and cross the street,

"C'mon, Dad, stay up with Mom.

Dad, they have those everywhere—you don't need to look at that."

You have to get them in a line.

"Mom? Dad?

Okay, let's cross here.

Come on, the light is changing.

Both of you, let's go, let's go, let's go."

"QUACK, QUACK, QUACK, QUACK."

It makes me crazy.

If they want to go out with me now I take them to a pond, let them paddle around.

I dry them off.

Take them home.

I think they're a lot happier that way.

Dad Trunks/Fashion Advice

The only thing to do in these places is the pool. My dad was always,

"How about a dip? You want to take a dip?"

I'd try and get out of it.

"I don't have a bathing suit."

My dad would go,

"You need trunks?

I got trunks.

Wear my trunks.

You're in the water. No one will see."

My dad didn't wear a bathing suit, he wore trunks.

You never see an old person with a new bathing suit.

I don't know why.

So I get in the water in this thing, and it's like floating . . . around me . . . somewhere.

Did you ever put on a bathing suit that you don't even know exactly

where you are inside the bathing suit?

You see somebody you know,

"No, I'm parasailing. I'm just waiting for the boat to come back."

My parents gave me 3 pieces of fashion advice:

"No one will see."

"It's what they're wearing."

and

"Today, anything goes."

Add all that up and you do not look good.

Mom Drives

My mother's in her 80s.

Lives in Florida.

Still driving.

I know. Crazy.

So, I've had her car fitted with a Cataract Windshield.

It's a one-foot-thick, curved glass, prescription windshield.

Everyone's head inside the car looks HUGE now.

People think it's a car full of sports mascots coming down the street.

She loves cruises.

My mother is on one constant cruise.

She takes cruises on land.

She took a cruise to Switzerland last year.

My mother told me she was leaving to take another cruise in two weeks.

I said,

"Where does this one go?"

I swear to god she said,

"I don't know."

They just want to go anywhere slowly.

I guess life goes by quickly and at the end you just want to stay under 12 mph.

Old Men Love Heat

Ever been to one of these retirement/resort communities to visit your parents?

And somehow end up in a hot tub with your father and 3 or 4 really old men?

And isn't that the best way to meet extremely old people?

Half-naked in tubs of hot bubbling water?

They get out, they look like an ad for gravity.

Old men can take tremendous amounts of heat.

Steam rooms, saunas, hot tubs, Jacuzzis.

They love heat.

Is Florida not hot and muggy enough for these people?

I'm sure if they ever try to land a man on the sun,

one of these old retired guys will be able to do it.

No space suit.

Just a terry-cloth jacket and a pair of flip-flops.

He'll sit there with a towel on his head going,

"Close the door.

In or out?

Come on.

You're letting all the heat off the sun."

Kotex Lady

I'm in the supermarket.

This is an absolute 100% true story.

Lady comes over to me and says,

"Excuse me, could you reach one of those purple boxes on the top shelf for me?"

I say, "Sure."

As I'm getting it, I notice it's Kotex.

Right at that moment, swear to god, she says,

"They're not for me, they're for my sister."

Okay. So, what am I supposed to say?

"Yeah, I bet they are . . .

I suppose those pantyhose are for your sister too, huh?

Listen, sugar, why don't you just cut the goody two-shoes,

'Kotex for my sister' crap

and get straight with me right now?

You never had a sister.

You never were a sister.

You're probably headed for the Summer's Eve right now.

I know about dames like you.

So, you score a few napkins, you move on to the next town and so what?

Maybe somebody, somewhere falls off a step ladder and breaks their neck.

What's the difference?

It's just another month to you.

Another napkin.

Another town left behind in confusion."

Got Old

We're pretty irrational when it comes to aging.

We want so badly for it not to happen to us.

We'll talk about other people like,

"Boy, he got old."

Just that particular guy.

Nobody else.

Like time is this mob syndicate, just singling out certain individuals.

"They got Joey. He's old."

Every birthday we say,

"Well . . . you're getting up there."

How long does that go on?

"Well, I'm 110 today."

"You're . . . there.

You—are—there—now."

Car-tastic

I love cars.

It's my favorite physical object.

I don't know why I think this.

My only theory is,

when you're driving:

You're outside and you're inside.

You're moving and you're completely still,

all at the same time.

New Car Steering Wheel

The main thing most people focus on when they look at a new car is the steering wheel.

They look at the outside, if they like that they get in it and hold the steering wheel.

They sit there, turn the wheel a few times and go,

"Yeah, this is a good car.

This car goes left OR right.

I need that feature."

Sneezing Driving

The thing that unnerves me most when I'm driving is when I've got to sneeze.

Because you know you're going to have to close your eyes for that split second.

And I'm afraid when I open them up, things may be different.

Like instead of looking at all taillights,

it's all headlights.

But there's nothing you can do.

You've just got to take that one last look and go,

"Don't anybody move!"

"Aaaaahhh . . ."

Traffic Lane Experts

I love the Lane Experts.

Constantly revising and updating their lane choice.

Always got the hand out the window.

"Can I get in there . . . ?

Can I get ahead of you . . . ?

Can I be part of your lane . . . ?

Ohh, you're in such a great lane . . ."

"Yeah, come on in, pal . . .

We're zooming over here.

This is the Secret Lane, nobody knows about it.

I'm letting you in, don't tell any of the other cars."

Leaving Car

There's really nothing you can do in traffic but try and see up ahead.

People are always *looking* in traffic.

"I think I see something.

Can you see anything?

Are they moving?"

I love when people get so frustrated in traffic that they just get right out of the car.

"What the hell is going on up there?"

They start walking right down the highway.

The whole car is absolutely worthless to them now.

They don't even want it.

It's the most expensive thing they own.

Just leave it.

Keys in it.

Engine running.

I love when this kind of idiotic male,

"I'm going to do something about this"

instinct kicks in.

"The hell with it.

It's not taking me anywhere anyway.

I can go places walking by myself.

That car was just holding me back."

Car Alarm

The car alarm is designed so that the car will behave as if it were a nervous, hysterical person.

Anyone goes near it, it just goes, "Waahaahaahaah!"

Lights flashing on and off, acting all crazy.

Not everyone wants to draw that much attention to themselves.

What if a car alarm was a little more subtle?

Somebody tries to break in the car and it goes,

"Uh, ahem . . . Ahem. Excuse me?"

I would like a car alarm like that.

Padded Ignition Key

My friend just got a new car and the ignition key has like a black rubber thing around it.

Now what kind of an amazing accident happens that your head goes forward.

But somehow you miss the steering wheel and hit just the key?

"Look out. Look out."

THOK.

"Oh . . . I hit the key.

But there was rubber on the end of it.

I'm okay . . ."

NYC Cab

The average New York cab ride is still one of the most exciting experiences in the city.

These guys take chances with your life for 5 bucks that you wouldn't take for 5 million.

First of all, the cars themselves are in good condition.

I've never once been in a New York cab that didn't have the "Check engine" light on.

I don't know if that means to check to see if you still have one, but it's always on.

I think because you're watching through the glass partition,

it's like it's all just happening on TV.

He's going 90 down a one-way,

you're like,

(laughing)

"Boy, I wouldn't try that in my car.

That seemed pretty dangerous."

He's up on two wheels on the sidewalk,

"This is a little crazy,

but I think we'll be on time at the restaurant.

. . . I've never seen an old lady jump straight up like that.

That's an impressive amount of spring for an older person . . ."

The dumbest thing you can think in the back of a taxicab is,

"Well, I'm sure the man knows what he's doing . . .

He's a professional cab driver.

He's got a license.

I can see it right there."

I don't even know what it takes to get a cab driver's license.

I think all you need is a face.

This seems to be their big qualification.

"No blank heads are allowed to drive cabs in New York City."

I believe that's an ordinance.

It also helps to have a name with like 8 consonants in a row.

And some of the letters in these names.

What is the "o" with the line through it?

You need a chart of the elements if you want to report the guy.

"Yes officer, his name was Amal and then the symbol for Boron."

Pickup Trucks

See a lot of pickup trucks in the Midwest.

What I have never seen is anything in the back of any of them.

Just eight people all crammed in the front going,

"Isn't this great . . . ?"

The only thing I ever see in the back is a big dog or a guy with no shirt on.

And they all talk about how someday they're going to get some shirts and ride up there in the front.

Sports Enthusiasm

I love sports.

But there is a certain critical line of sports enthusiasm.

Where it can get a little uncomfortable . . .

Where people start to act like they are *in* the game.

They say things like, "We won! We won!"

"No, *they* won.

You watched.

Just calm down.

I saw the whole game.

You did not play.

It's one of the main reasons they won."

People get into it like,

if you *beat* the team from the other city,

you *win* that city.

It's yours.

You go in their stores, take anything you want.

Rooting for Laundry

Love my team.

Even though we know, of course, they're not really teams.

We block that out.

We have to.

Players go to different teams.

Teams move from city to city.

The uniform is the only constant.

Why am I yelling,

"Go, New York, go!"

at a guy from East Illinois that'll be playing in Phoenix next season?

That's sports.

The uniform is the only constant.

We just want our clothes to beat the clothes from the other city.

We're rooting for laundry.

That's really all sports is.

If a player leaves your team, then comes back and plays against your team?

The hostility.

"Booo . . . Different shirt."

Exact same human being.

"I hate this guy.

He's in a different shirt."

The Silver Medal

I think the worst thing in the Olympics is the Silver.

You win the Gold you feel good.

You win the Bronze you feel,

"At least I got something . . ."

But the Silver is like,

"Congratulations, you ALMOST won.

Of all the losers, you were the best.

You're the Number One Loser.

No one lost ahead of you."

I don't know how they live with that the rest of their lives.

Because you've got to tell the story.

Everyone wants to hear the story.

"Wow . . . Silver medal?

Congratulations!

That's impressive.

Did you lose by a lot or a little?

Did you trip?

Did you not hear the gun go off?"

And it's horrible how they can lose by just a few hundredths of a second . . .

So, each moment that amount of time goes by he must think,

"It was just from 'there to there.'

That's how much . . .

It was just th—.

I trained. I worked out.

I never had a date.

I never had a drink.

I never had a beer.

I was doing push-ups when I was a fetus.

I traveled halfway around the world.

The uniform . . . everybody I knew in my whole life was there . . . my parents

The gun went off, got to the end, and then it was just, 'tht'

—and I lost.

That much.

That was it.

Just from 'now to now.'

'N— to n—'

Just 'nt—' and it was over.

It was a photo finish.

(in profile moves head a tiny amount)

"It was Gold . . . Silver . . . Bronze . . . Dead Last."

(head slightly in front)

"Greatest guy in the world."

(head slightly behind)

"Never heard of him."

"If I had a pimple on the end of my nose,

I would've won."

The Platforms of Humiliation

Then they have the award ceremony with those Platforms of Humiliation.

"Because not only are you not as good an athlete as the winner, we want to give the impression that you're a much smaller person too."

(Second-place winner looking up at first-place winner)

"Well, con . . . grat . . . u . . . la . . . tions . . ."

Why don't they get rid of the platforms,

let the second and third person lie naked with their hands and feet tied, the winner can stand on their faces?

Maybe then it would be clear enough.

Biathlon

The Biathlon is a favorite of mine.

Biathlon combines skiing and shooting a gun.

How many alpine snipers are into this?

Seems like two totally unrelated things.

It's like combining swimming and strangle a guy.

You swim a lap,

throttle a guy,

kick turn,

back across the pool.

Platform Diving

On the other end of the Olympic spectrum you have like, Platform Diving.

Where the judging is so critical, it's too depressing to watch.

If the diver makes too big a splash going in the water all the judges are like,

"What the hell was that?

That was the dive?

Well, that's just no good at all.

Look, one of the drops landed right here on my shirt.

All the flipping, turning and twisting in the air means nothing now.

No, sir. Not if you're going to make a splash like that.

He's just going to have to learn to slow down before he hits that water."

The Involuntary Luge

The luge is another great Olympic event.

It's on the bobsled run.

But there's no sled.

It's just Bob.

I think it's the only sport I've ever seen

that if you had people competing in it against their will,

it would be basically the same thing.

If they were just grabbing people off the street.

(fighting back) "Hey, hey, hey . . . I don't want to be in that."

Then strap them to the thing and shoot them down the course.

We would have no way of knowing.

He's got the helmet on, so we wouldn't hear the screaming.

"Sorry, buddy, you're in the luge."

World record.

Didn't even want to do it.

They should try it in the next Olympics.

Call it,

the Involuntary Luge.

Pedestrian Rodeo

What do I do for entertainment in my spare time?

One thing I really enjoy is to see someone on an icy sidewalk slip a little and almost fall.

I don't want them to really fall.

I just love that, "Whoa, whoa . . . ," look on their face.

People will actually say "whoa."

There are no horses anywhere in the area.

It's impossible not to say, "whoa."

It's Pedestrian Rodeo and the object is to stay on as long as you can.

It's amazing how just a slight little loss of footing erases a lifetime of building confidence.

You see straight through to this totally insecure toddler that just wants Mommy.

Then just as quick they snap right back to secure, stable person again.

"No one saw.

Just keep walking . . .

No one knows who I really am inside."

Call Waiting

I called the phone company the other day to see if I could get that Call Waiting thing.

I love that thing.

You're talking with somebody.

Click the button.

Get a new person.

The other person has to wait.

Sealed inside the Call Waiting Isolation Chamber.

(Hands on glass)

There's nothing they can do.

Only you can get them out.

Ever see people's faces on Call Waiting?

It's like their soul has left their body.

"Are you talking with someone?"

"I don't know . . . I was . . .

I don't know . . . what's happening . . ."

The ultimate phone accessory would be

if they had a thing that makes your phone immune to Call Waiting.

So people try to get rid of you,

but they can't.

They click the thing and you're just,

"I'm still here, Fred.

I've got Call Waiting Kryptonite.

Now why don't you take your hand away from that button and listen to what I have to say?"

Phone Machine

Have you ever called someone up and you're disappointed when they answer?

You wanted the machine.

You're totally thrown off.

You go, "Oh . . . I . . . didn't know you'd be there.

I just wanted to leave a message saying, 'Sorry I missed you.' "

So because of the phone machine,

what you can have is two people that don't really ever want to talk, and the phone machine is like this relationship respirator keeping these marginal, brain-dead relationships alive.

Why do we do this?

Because when we come home we want to see that little flashing red light.

And go, "All right, messages."

People need that.

It's very important for human beings to feel they are popular and

well-liked amongst a large group of people that they have no interest in.

I love my phone machine.

I wish I was a phone machine.

I wish if I saw somebody on the street I didn't want to talk to I could just go,

"Excuse me, I'm not here right now. If you just leave a message, I can walk away."

I also have a cordless phone, but I don't like that much.

Because you can't slam down a cordless phone. You get mad at somebody on a real phone,

"You can't talk to me like that!"

BANG, it's over.

But a cordless phone—

"You can't talk to me like that!

All right now, let me just find that little thing to turn this off

. . . Just hang on, I'm hanging up on you."

And when the phone machine breaks,

people scoop them up and carry them in their arms like sick children.

They yell at befuddled repairmen,

"What do you mean there's nothing you can do?"

The phone machine is like your little message fisherman.

You come in the door, "How was the catch today? They biting?"

I'm sure somewhere someone has returned a phone machine,

like a bad lure, because it didn't get enough calls.

I would say the concept behind the car phone, and the phone machine,

the speaker phone, the airline phone, the portable phone, the pay phone, the cordless phone, the multi-line phone, the phone pager, the call waiting, the call forwarding,

call conferencing, speed dialing, direct dialing, and the redialing,

is that we all have absolutely nothing to say,

and we've got to talk to someone about it right now.

Cannot wait another second!

You're at home you're on the phone.

You're in the car you're making calls.

You get to work, "Any messages for me?"

You've got to give people a chance to miss you a little bit.

Cell Phone Speech

Why does everyone talk like the person on the other phone

is trapped in a submarine on the ocean floor?

"You're breaking up . . . Hang on . . . !"

"Breaking up"?

What is this, Apollo 13?

You're at the mall, take it easy.

You're talking to somebody at the food court Cinnabon . . .

That you can see from the escalator as you're coming down.

Paint Apartment

I've been in the same apartment for years.

I just keep painting it.

The wall outlets are just a mound of paint with two slots in it.

It looks like a pig is trying to push his way through from the other side.

And every time I paint it I think,

"Well, it's just a little bit smaller now."

I realize it's just the thickness of the paint, but still . . .

Each time, it's coming in on me a little bit more.

I think eventually someone will open the front door

and it'll be just a solid white block with an eye.

People will go, "Wow, that guy painted too much."

Toaster Room

I don't cook.

I have a kitchen.

I've been in it.

To me, a kitchen is just a big room to hold a toaster.

That's the way I think of my apartment.

Bedroom, Living Room, Toaster Room.

Winter—I'll turn that dial thing up.

Make the toast darker.

Summer—I turn it down.

With the sun and the hot weather I like it a little more on the light side.

That's as into cuisine as I get.

My other big home cooking interest is using the right size plate.

I don't like using too big a plate.

I'm not exactly sure what it's a waste of.

I guess having to wash unutilized plate area.

I'm wetting it, soaping it up, rinsing it, drying it.

And it wasn't needed for anything.

Also, when I'm making my bed and I tuck in one side of the sheet I stay bent over as I move to tuck in the other side.

Why stand up and then bend over again?

When I finish with my cereal, I put the bowl away with the spoon in it.

Why go to a separate drawer to get a spoon every morning?

How often am I going to use that bowl and not need the spoon that goes with it?

I'll worry about that situation when I'm faced with it.

Diet

Everybody wants to know everybody's diet.

"You look okay, what do you eat?"

Here's mine:

I eat pretty good.

But if I'm hungry and there's something in front of me, I eat that.

When I get back to my hotel late at night after doing a show,

if there's a room service tray in the hallway and there's a roll on it,

that doesn't look too bad . . .

I would and have eaten it.

I figure, what are the odds that somebody in a hotel room would go,

"Hey, before we put the tray out, let's inject a roll with poison, leave it in the hall,

in case there's a comic coming back to his room at two o'clock in the morning—we can kill him."

Restaurant Check Timing

I have never liked the standard restaurant

"Check at the end of the meal system."

Because money is a very different thing before and after you eat.

When you're hungry, money means nothing . . .

You're like the ruler of an empire.

CLAP, CLAP,

"We must have more appetizers, more drinks!

Little fried things in the shape of a stick or a ball.

This will be The Greatest Meal of Our Lives."

Then after the meal when you're full,

you can't remember ever being hungry ever in your life.

You see people walking in the restaurant, you can't believe it.

"Why are these people coming in here now?

I'm so full.

How could THEY eat?"

You've got the pants undone, napkins destroyed, cigarette butt in the mashed potatoes.

You never want to see food again as long as you live.

And that's when the check comes.

This is why people are always mystified by the check.

"What is this?

How could this be?"

They start passing it around the table.

"Does this look RIGHT to you?

We're not hungry now, why are we buying all this food?"

Nightclub of Clothes

So, I assume the clothes I'm looking at are the best of what was left in your closet?

They're the lucky ones.

They got picked.

They got to go out.

Anything you're not wearing right now is just home, hoping to get picked tomorrow.

Shirt is like,

"He never picks me.

Used to wear me all the time.

Lost a button . . ."

It's a lot of waiting.

In the closet.

In the hamper.

In the drawer.

That's why laundry day's the most exciting day.

The washing machine is like a nightclub for clothes.

It's dark, bubbles happening, they're all kind of dancing around in there.

Shirt grabs the underwear, "Come on, babe, let's go."

You come by,

open the lid, they all freeze.

"Would you close the door, please?

This is actually a private club . . .

We have a dress code.

It's 'Clothes Only.'

Nothing is allowed to be on anyone."

Sometimes I take the clothes out, they're all twisted together.

I don't even want to know what happened.

Dry Cleaning

I've got to go to the dry cleaner tomorrow and have a fight with that guy.

I don't even know what it's going to be about.

But that's why you go to the dry cleaner.

So you can walk in and say,

"Well, it's ruined."

And then he can say,

"We're not responsible."

Let's get one thing straight about dry cleaning right now.

It doesn't exist. There's no such thing as dry cleaning.

My first question is,

"What the hell is dry cleaning fluid?"

There's no dry fluids.

There's no way of cleaning with dry, washing with dry, or doing anything with dry.

Dry itself is nothing. You can't use it. You can't do anything with it.

It's not there. It doesn't exist.

We walk into these places with the big signs out front, "Dry Cleaning," and for some reason never question how they were able to put this absurd concept over on us.

If I gave you a filthy shirt and said, "I want this immaculate. No liquids!"

What are you going to do? Shake it? Tap it? Blow on it?

———

You almost can't get something dirty with dry, let alone clean it.

And "One-Hour Martinizing."

You know what I think One-Hour Martinizing is?

I think they just put the clothes in plastic and give it right back to you.

That's One-Hour Martinizing.

You can get One-Second Martinizing if you want it.

I wonder if the dry cleaners ever wear the clothes?

Why not?

Imagine bumping into your dry cleaner at a party and he's wearing your sweater?

(loud whisper)

"Hey!!

What the hell are you doing?!

That better be ready by tomorrow."

Dry Clean Only

"Dry clean only" is definitely the only warning label that human beings actually respect.

They'll look at cigarettes,

"This will give you cancer, kill you, your kids, your parents, everyone."

"No, screw it. I'll do whatever the hell I want."

"Don't drink this medicine and operate heavy machinery."

"Ahh, who cares? Glug, glug, glug . . .

That's for people that don't know what the hell they're doing. I'm a pro."

But if you have something that's dry clean only,

and somebody goes to put it in the washing machine,

"Don't put it in the washing machine!

It's dry clean only!

Are you crazy? You out of your mind?"

Gentle Cycle

When I do wash I always like to use the gentle cycle.

Sounds so much more humane.

Or the gentle/gentle cycle.

You could put a baby in there.

Won't hurt it.

I don't know what the machine's doing in there that's so gentle.

But it's very private.

Because you pick up the lid on the machine, it stops immediately.

"Would you close that please?

Can't you see I'm in the middle of a very delicate cycle?"

Engaged

I got engaged about 10 or so years ago.

Didn't want to get married, that was the closest I got.

I can tell you this, if you're engaged and you don't want to get married . . .

It's a little tense.

Being engaged is like being on just that first part of the roller coaster where you're going

up and up and you have no idea what the rest of the ride is.

You just hear that, "click tick, click tick, click tick."

"Boy, this thing goes up pretty high . . ."

You get to the top, they give you a ring and a piece of cake and you just go,

"Aah-aah . . . we're marrr-iiieeeddd."

Commitment

Why is commitment such a problem for a man?

I think that for some reason when a man is driving down that freeway of love,

the woman he's involved with is like an exit.

But he doesn't want to get off there.

He wants to keep driving.

And the woman is like,

"Look, gas, food, lodging.

That's our exit.

That's everything we need to be happy. . . . Get off here, now!"

But the man focuses on the sign underneath that says,

"Next exit twenty-seven miles."

And he goes, "I think I can make it."

Sometimes he can, sometimes he can't.

Sometimes the car ends up on the side of the road.

Hood up and smoke pouring out of the engine.

He's sitting on the curb all alone.

"I guess I didn't realize how many miles I was racking up."

Mozzarella Relationships

There's no easy way to break off any relationship.

It's like the mozzarella cheese on a good slice of pizza.

It just gets thinner and longer but it doesn't want to break.

One way to end the relationship is adultery.

You can't just "have" an adultery.

You must commit adultery.

And of course, you can't commit adultery unless you have a commitment.

So you must make the commitment before you can even think about committing it.

There's no commit without the commit.

Then you can get caught, get divorced, lose your mind, and they have you committed.

Cheating

Some people actually cheat on the people that they're cheating with.

Which is like holding up a bank and then turning to the guy you're robbing it with and going,

"All right, now give me everything you have, too."

Why stop at just what's in the bank?

Friends After Dating

I think that if you've had a relationship with someone

and you try to become friends afterward, it's very difficult.

Because you know each other too well.

It's like two magicians trying to entertain each other.

The one goes, "Look, a rabbit."

The other goes, "So? . . . I believe this is your card."

"Look, why don't we just saw each other in half and call it a night, okay?"

Baby Life

My sister's having a baby.

Everyone gets excited when a baby is born.

Except the baby.

Because it's no fun being a baby.

They don't know their bodies are going to grow.

They're born, they look down, they think,

"Well, I guess this is the body I've got.

You've got to be kidding me.

Tiny hands, giant head, lousy plumbing.

Where am I going to find a tie that long?"

At 6 months old they immediately put you in charge of complicated toys you have no idea how to operate.

I had a Busy Box in my playpen.

All those knobs, buttons, switches.

I'm working this thing.

I didn't know it's not connected to anything.

I'd make in my pants, everybody gets upset.

I'd think, "I got this thing set way too high."

Every meal, they sit you down, strap a bib on you.

You think, "Alright, lobster."

And you don't get it.

Bachelor Party and Bridal Shower

I have a friend who's about to get married.

They're having the bachelor party and the bridal shower the same day.

So, it's conceivable that while the girl's friends are giving her sexy lingerie,

the guy could be at a strip club watching a table dancer in the exact same outfit.

That's a special moment.

Bad Gifts

To me, there's no better gift than a paperweight to express to someone, "I refuse to put any thought into this at all."

And where are these people working that the papers are just blowing right off of their desks?

Is their office screwed to the back of a flatbed truck going down the highway?

Are they typing in the crow's nest of a clipper ship?

What do you need a paperweight for?

Where's the wind coming from?

Touch Face Relationship

If you're in a relationship, there's pressure.

That's a fact of life.

You can see it whenever you ask someone about their relationship.

Because they are immediately a little nervous,

the first thing they will do is touch their face.

"So how is it going with Judy?"

(scratching chin)

"Not bad."

And the higher up on their face they go,

the worse the relationship is getting.

"Heard you're having some problems."

(touching forehead)

"Not really."

"Are you going to break up?"

(pushing hair back on head)

"Yeah, we've got to break up.

I can't go any higher on my HEAD."

Sperm and Egg

The sperm and the egg seem to be role models for how men and women act in real life.

If you could look down at the earth from altitude and watch men behaving on a weekend night,

I think they'd look very much like sperm.

All disorganized,

overly energetic,

awkward,

bumping into their friends,

swimming in the wrong direction.

"I was first."

"Let me through."

"You're on my tail."

"Hey, this was my spot."

We're like the 3 Billion Stooges.

And The Egg is very cool . . .

"Well, who's it going to be?

I can divide . . .

I can wait a month.

Do any of you have it together . . . ?"

Pet Monkey

My next-door neighbor just got a pet monkey.

Now there's a lot of different animals you can get if you want a pet.

But I would say once you find yourself at the monkey level . . .

Just have a kid . . .

You're soo close.

It's one more little step.

When you need a pet that can roller skate and smoke cigars, maybe it's time to think about a family.

It's not a good pet anyway.

He's got a leash for it like he's going to walk it.

You can't walk a monkey.

Any place a monkey has to be . . .

They just, "ya" and he's there.

So the guy tries to walk him and it's like "ya" he's on the wall.

"Ya" he's on your head. He's on a pole.

There's so much tension in monkeys.

That face skin is pulled so tight.

When you come that close to being the dominant species on the planet and you don't make it.

You feel pressure all the time after that.

"I can't believe how close we were.

We got the thumbs and everything."

―――――

It's not like a dog.

A dog is great on a leash.

Total acceptance.

Give it a good yank, his body flips up in the air.

He looks around like,

"I'm sure I had that coming to me for something.

I don't know what I did.

But I'm a dog, I understand my position."

Monkeys just look right at you.

I hate when he leaves me alone with it.

Have you ever been alone with a monkey?

You sit there looking at each other eye to eye . . .

There's a feeling like,

"Did we go to high school together or something?

You look so familiar . . .

Did you go out for gymnastics?

I'd remember that.

You would be outstanding at that."

Date End

How do you say goodbye on a date when you never want to see this person again for the rest of your life?

No matter how much you want to be nice . . .

Everything you say is a lie.

"See you around . . .

See you . . . around.

If I'm around and you're around I'll probably see you in that area.

You'll be around other people, though.

You won't be around me.

You'll just be around."

"Take care now.

Take care . . .

Now.

Because I'm not going to be taking care of you.

So, take care of yourself.

Starting . . . now."

Shower World

I've got to take a shower.

I'm not dirty.

I just need that break.

The shower is the only real break you get in life.

When you're in the shower, it's like you've left the world.

When you're asleep, they can bother you.

But not when you're in the shower.

People call on the phone,

other people have to answer . . .

"Yeah, no . . .

There's no way anyone can reach him.

He's in the shower.

I'm sorry.

There's nothing anyone can do."

And when you get out of the shower you're still not available.

"I'm going to have to call you back.

I just got out of the shower.

Don't you understand?

I JUST GOT OUT.

I was naked, singing, rubbing myself all over.

I'm not back to reality.

I was living a complete fantasy life."

Shower Radio

Someone gave me a shower radio as a present.

Great gift.

What better place to dance than naked, on a slick surface, next to a glass door?

The whole point of the shower is nothing matters when you're in there.

Unless someone flushes a toilet, that matters a great deal.

You ever do that?

There's a sense of *power.*

You move this little handle and down the hall 30 feet away, in another room

someone screams like they're in an electric chair.

It's like voodoo.

You call people in,

"You know Ed's in the shower, right?

Watch this, we can control his whole life right from here."

(pushes handle)

"Aaaaaahh!"

(pushes handle just a little)

"Aa"

It's a very sensitive control.

I'm Naked

I don't belong to a health club.

I have a strict limit on the number of naked men I need to see in one day.

Zero is my limit.

When you're naked anyplace outside your own home,

there is absolutely no mental awareness of anything other than, "I'm naked."

You walk from the locker to the shower, all you're thinking is,

"I'm naked. I'm naked. I'm naked. I'm naked."

You meet someone, you go,

"Hi, I'm naked.

Yes, that's my name, Naked.

My first name?

Butt.

Butt Naked."

Actually, for years I've never been sure whether it's butt naked or buck naked.

Some people say "butt," some people say "buck."

Buck Naked sounds like some nude rodeo cowboy or something.

"Howdy, I'm Buck Naked.

Have you seen my clothes?

I just finished riding and I'd like to put my pants back on.

I left them hanging over the fence.

If this is somebody's idea of a joke I don't think it's very funny."

Women Try On

When women shop, they don't try on clothes.

They get BEHIND clothes.

They leave it on the hanger.

Hold in the waist.

Cock the head.

And stick one leg WAY out.

They need to know,

"If someday I'm one-legged living on a planet at a 45-degree angle,

what am I going to wear?"

I've never seen a man put his head in the neck of a suit and go,

"Yeah, this is perfect, I'll take this suit.

Wait, let me see how it looks when I'm dancing.

Put some shoes at the bottom of the pants.

Okay. Now,

move the shoes

move the shoes

move—the—shoes . . ."

The Chicks and the Checks

I'm in the supermarket.

There are two women in front of me on the checkout line.

And I like that because it is, after all,

the "Checkout" line.

So one of them, her total was $3,

the other one $8.

They both of course choose to pay by the use of the . . . check.

And you know how you are on the supermarket line anyway . . .

You see the person in front of you pull out a check and you're . . .

("Oh my god" . . . face)

Have you noticed that women write out a lot more checks than men?

Where is your money?

You have automobiles.

You're all always wearing nice shoes.

There must be SOME money somewhere.

Where is it?

Ladies, if you don't have 3 dollars, do not go out of the house.

But the fact is,

if it's a woman in front of you using the check,

you will not be waiting long.

Because women write out so many checks,

they are so fluent in the check writing process . . .

It's like two seconds, and they're out of there.

The checkbook is the one thing in their purse they can find immediately.

Most difficult thing for women to find in their purse?

Keys.

No idea where the keys are.

They just keep digging around. In there . . .

They end up having to dump the bag out on the floor . . .

(raking motion)

Rake through it.

But the checkbook, they got that.

That comes out of a holster.

(quick draw from holster)

"Who do I make it out to?"

"Here's my I.D."

They don't have to ask the date.

They know it.

They've already written 6 checks that morning.

You don't see men doing that.

Men are like,

". . . Hang on a second.

I'm trying to get the perforation started.

I DON'T WANT TO RIP IT.

It's the first check in the book.

If I rip it, there'll be this little triangle of paper hanging down and I'll have to look at that for three months."

Men don't like checks.

Men like cash.

Money.

"I have money.

This is money right here.

I made this money and I'm directly associated with it.

You need more, no problem."

(peeling off a roll)

A check is a very emasculating experience.

It's like a note from your mother.

That says,

"I don't have any money,

but if you contact these people . . .

I'm sure they'll stick up for me.

I really don't understand how this works.

You see, I gave my money to these people here . . .

(points to check)

And they gave me these . . .

(looks sheepish)

I put my name on it.

And the amount of money that I wish I had.

Is that worth anything at all?"

You have to beg this guy to take the check.

Small stores always like to have bad checks very proudly
displayed on the wall behind the register.

Like this proves them right about something.

"You see?

You can't trust people.

Oh, I tried to trust people.

Look at what happened."

And even if he takes the check and trusts you.

How much do you trust him in return?

Not very much.

Because when you write out the check

After the dollar amount,

you always put that long line all the way down to the end,

so he can't write in,

"And 100 million dollars too!"

If they can write it in, I think the law is

I have to pay that.

Men's Physical World

The man's world is the physical world.

Men like building, fixing and working on things.

Or being around other men that are building, fixing or working on things.

Men must control and dominate physical things.

Because we know that women are pretty much controlling everything else.

Ever see how if one man is doing some kind of job with tools out in his driveway other men in the neighborhood are magnetically drawn to it?

They look through the drapes,

"I think Jim's working on something over there . . . I better get over there."

Men hear the sound of the drill, it's like a dog whistle.

"Whhhrrr . . . (head cock-turn)"

They just start wandering up like zombies.

They don't help the guy.

They don't want to do any work.

We just want to be in the area where work is being done.

Asking stupid questions like,

"What are you using, a Phillips head there?

That's a good screwdriver, the Phillips."

That's why construction sites have to have those wood panel fences around it.

Just to keep the men out.

They cut those little holes for us.

So we can stick our heads in and see what the hell's going on.

Talk to other men that have stuck their heads in.

"Is that a Phillips down there?"

"Yeah, looks like he's using a Phillips."

Superhero Men

Women,

the thing you've got to understand about men is,

men think we can accomplish virtually anything of a physical nature that needs to be done.

Every man secretly believes inside his own mind

that he is a low-level superhero.

This is the true inner nature of men.

I'm not even really supposed to be telling you this.

When men are growing up and we're reading about Batman, Superman, Spider-Man.

These are not fantasies to us.

These are our options.

All men think,

"If I had to swing from a rope.

Crash through a window.

And beat up a room full of bad guys.

I would probably somehow be able to do it.

In the meantime, I'm going to straighten up the garage.

Because that's pretty important too."

You ever see a guy with a mattress on the roof of his car, driving down the highway?

Without fail, he's got his hand out the window, holding the mattress.

This is classic, male, idiot superhero thinking.

This moron believes that if the wind catches this huge rectangle at 70 mph,

"I got it. I got it . . .

I am using MY ARM."

Men's Minds

Men love looking at women.

We think, "We don't understand them.

We better keep an eye on them."

———

I know I will not understand women.

I know I will never be able to understand how a woman can take boiling hot wax,

pour it on her upper thighs, rip the hair out by the root.

And still be afraid of a spider.

I'm not spending any more time working on that.

And I know women don't understand men.

I know there are women that are looking at me right now going,

"I wonder what goes on in that little brain of his?

I bet you I could manipulate that brain."

I bet you could.

Men spend half our lives walking down the street going,

"Hey, there's a couple of girls."

"What are they doing?"

"I don't know . . ."

"Did you see that other girl?"

"No, I missed her."

"Ooooohhhh."

I don't know what that sound means but it is one of our highest ratings.

And I'm sure women probably wonder,

"What are men thinking anyway?"

You really want to know what men are thinking?

Because I can tell you what men are thinking.

You know what we're thinking?

Nothing.

We're not thinking anything.

Not a god damned thing.

We're thinking,

"We want women."

That's it.

That is the only clear thought any of us has ever had our entire lives.

The next step after that, we have absolutely no idea what to do about it.

That's why we're honking car horns, making kissing noises out the window.

These are the best ideas we've had so far.

We're trying to come up with some new programs but it's not easy when your mind's a blank.

The car horn honk is really the unbelievable one to me.

We've all seen this.

What do you expect the woman to do?

Kick off the heels, start running after the car?

Finally catch it.

"Excuse me, was that for me?

Well, it's a good thing you honked.

I had no idea how you felt."

———

Why do men behave in these ways?

Why are we rude, obnoxious, getting drunk,

falling down, peeling rubber, making kissing noises out the window?

Why are we like this?

I know what you ladies are thinking.

"No, not my guy. I'm working with him, he's coming along."

No, he's not.

He's not coming anywhere.

We men know, no matter how poorly we behave,

it seems we will somehow end up with women anyway.

Look around this room.

Look at all the men you see with lovely women.

Do you think these are special men?

Gifted men?

One-of-a-kind men?

No.

They're the same jerks and idiots that I'm talking about.

They're doing just fine.

Men, as an organization, are getting more women

than any other group working anywhere in the world today.

Wherever women are, we have men looking into the situation right now.

We explored the Earth looking for women.

We even went to the moon just to see if there were any women there.

That's why we brought that little car.

Why would you bring a car, unless there's some chance of going on a date?

What the hell were they doing with a car on the god damn moon?

You're on the moon already!

Isn't that far enough?

There is no more male idea in the history of the universe than,

"Why don't we fly up to the moon and drive around?"

Phone Control/Sex Control

Woman called me up the other day, asked me out on a date.

I'll tell you guys, I don't know if this kind of thing is as good for us as it seems on the surface.

It changes the balance of power in the dating world.

Which is, women have sex control, men have phone control.

In the beginning of a relationship, women control all sexual decisions.

Who, where, when, type, style, duration, and rate of progress.

The basic conversation between every man and every woman on every date

is the man saying,

"I would like to have sex right now."

And the woman saying,

"Well, we're not."

Sometimes the woman will give the man an excuse.

She doesn't really have to.

She can say anything.

"I'm tired.

I'm not tired.

You're tired.

Someone in Italy is tired."

Anything.

Now, on the other side, the power that men have is phone control.

That's why we try so hard to get your number.

"Did you get her number?"

"I talked to her, she said she might give me the number."

"You should get the number."

"I'm trying to get the number."

We want that number.

That's phone control.

Now, we can call.

If we want to call.

We might call.

We might not call.

We might wait.

You might wonder.

You might worry.

But now, if women are calling, then they have phone control too.

And they already had sex control.

So what do men have now in the dating world?

Nothing.

We're just driving and paying now.

You might as well put us in a baby seat in the back of the car.

That's how much power we have.

Give us a foam rubber steering wheel with a red button in the middle.

"Beep, beep. Hey, you missed the theater. Beep. That's where the movie is. Beep, beep."

And even though women are getting phone control,

they're not giving us any sex control in exchange.

You can't give men sex control.

That wouldn't be good.

Women would never see the inside of a restaurant for the rest of their lives.

We'd show up at your house with food.

We'd drive by restaurants, you'd go,

"What's that?"

"It's a clubhouse you don't need to know anything about it. We're going home."

We'd trade in all the sports cars.

Just drive those aluminum snack vans with the sides that swing open.

Who needs a sports car if you've got sex control?

You just need a quick bite to eat, later.

The
Nineties

I remember so well sitting there with Larry David at our pitch meeting for *Seinfeld* at NBC.

And I remember saying,

"We want the show to be about how a comedian gets his material."

In my head I'm thinking,

"What a load of nonsense this is.

Is anyone dumb enough to believe what I'm saying?

But it does sound good.

I think that's what this meeting is about . . .

Just say stuff that sounds good . . ."

Then I threw in some bit I had about waitresses in coffee shops walking around

with a pot of coffee in each hand looking for people that had coffee, trying to give them more coffee.

That got a laugh.

And the next thing I knew I had a TV series.

———

"How a comedian gets his material."

Please.

If you could go back to any time and place in history,

would you go back to Van Gogh in an art store buying the paint??

NO. Of course not.

What the hell is that?

You would go back to watch him painting!!

That's what you want to see.

And that's what you're seeing in a stand-up set.

The artist painting the picture right now, right in front of me.

That's why it's so compelling.

It's happening right now.

Why he's doing it and where he got the ideas are stupid questions.

———

The stand-up stuff I did for the TV series was not at all the way I liked working.

I love working really slowly and taking a really long time figuring out what I want the bit to be.

In the series I had to work really fast and had no time.

I do think because Larry and I approached the show as stand-ups is why the comedy works so well.

There is a stand-up rhythm to the dialogue

and a stand-up mindset to the story lines.

———

When we finished the series the celebration was much more like the over-drained marathoner than the sprinter.

They do one weak little fist pump, not even above their head

and then right into the aluminum blanket.

The look on their face is,

"Obviously, that was worth it. But also . . . a ridiculously long run."

First Aid

What do you think First Aid was like hundreds of years ago?

They had no medicine, no drugs, no technology, no equipment.

Basically, they were there first.

That was it. That was the whole First Aid.

They sat with you, that's all they could do.

"Can you help me in any way?"

"No. But we were the first ones here.

Did you see our truck?

'First Aid,' that's our motto.

We do nothing. But we show up before anybody."

Museum Security Guards

Do the security guards in the art museums

really ever stop anybody from taking the paintings?

Are they going up to thieves,

"Hey, hey, hey, where do you think you're going with that Cézanne?"

Look at the job that this man is hired to do.

He's getting five dollars an hour to protect millions of dollars of priceless art, with a light mocha brown uniform and a *USA Today*.

That's all he's got.

Crooks must look at this guy and go,

"Alright, all we've got to do is get past the folding chair and the thermos of coffee

and we can get a Rembrandt."

Men's Jobs

Women have to like the job of the guy they're with.

They don't like the job, they don't like the guy.

Men know this.

That's why we've invented the phony, bogus names for the jobs that we have.

"Right now, I'm managing regional development systems.

Doing research, production, overseeing and administrating, assistant to the supervisor.

Consulting on a lot of things in the area.

I'm out of work.

Can I be honest with you?

I have no job at all."

But if a man is physically attracted to a woman it's not really important to him what her job is.

"Slaughterhouse, really?

That sounds great.

Must be interesting with all the blood.

So you take a big meat cleaver and are just lopping their heads right off?

Amazing.

Anyway, why don't you wash up

and we'll grab a couple of cheeseburgers and catch a movie?"

Psychiatrist

Then there's the psychiatrist.

Why is it that with the psychiatrist every hour is only fifty minutes?

What do they do with that ten minutes that they have left?

Do they just sit there going,

"Boy, that guy was crazy.

I couldn't believe the things he was saying.

What a nut . . .

Who's coming in next?

Oh no, another head case."

Money

I have not done well as an investor in things.

People always tell me, "You should have your money working for you."

I've decided, I think I'll do the work, I'm going to let my money relax.

Because who knows what your money has been through before it got to you?

Maybe it's been working. Maybe it's tired. Maybe that's why it left where it was.

Maybe if I'm nice to it, it'll stay with me.

I hate when they call up to check if your credit card is good.

I always feel like they're talking about me.

"You won't believe what he's buying now.

It's some kind of yellow thing.

I don't even know what it is, we've never sold one before.

Get down here right away, I'll try and stall him . . ."

Office Space

To me, the most annoying thing about the couple of times that I've worked in offices

is that when you show up in the morning

you say "hi" to everyone.

And then for some reason, you have to continue to greet these people all day every time you see them.

You walk in at the start of the day,

"Morning, Bill. Morning, Bob. How are you doing?"

"Fine."

Ten minutes later you see them in the hall, again you say, "Hey, how you doing?"

I already know how he's doing.

I just saw him.

But you've got to keep saying something each time you pass.

So you keep coming up with different little greetings.

Nicknames . . . "Jimboo."

You do the little smile with the small head/eyebrow raise.

The almost imperceptible beneath-the-breath "Hey" with a half-smile.

If it's a narrow passageway, you have "Excuse me."

But it has to have a very friendly, singsong quality.

You kind of go up a note on the "me."

When walking by a group of 3 or more men, "Gentlemen."

To confer a misplaced air of sophistication.

People like any mention of "the weekend."

"Good weekend?"

"Weekend's almost here . . ."

We should all agree that we're just going to say,

"Acknowledge," as we pass people in the halls.

You know, just walk by,

"Acknowledge."

"Acknowledge."

We'll become Vulcans for four seconds

and not have to wrack our brains every time we just want to go to the bathroom.

The Casual Heil

I was watching a World War Two Nazi movie.

The Nazis in those movies seemed to have two different "Heil"s.

They had the regular arm-extended "Heil" that they would do at parades and stuff.

And then, around the offices, they had this casual "Heil"

where they would just kind of show their palm.

They come in the office, "Yeah, Heil, how are you?

Is the kid back with the coffee yet? Are you finished with the copier?

Yeah, world domination, Aryan race, whose donuts are those?

Hey Heil, nice to see you. How's the Holocaust going . . . ?

Mind if I take the last jelly?"

Malls

Every mall has a Hoffritz knife store in it.

I'm sorry, but this has got to be kind of a scary place to work.

They put like a 16-year-old girl behind the counter.

And all day people are coming in saying things like,

"I need knives. I need more knives.

Do you have any bigger knives? Sharper knives?

I need a big, long, sharp knife.

That's what I'm in the market for.

Do you have one with hooks and ridges on the blade?

That's the kind of knife I'm looking for.

I need one I can throw, and I need another one I can just hack away with.

Do you have anything like that?"

Really Bad Traffic

The *complete dead stop* is, of course, the ultimate traffic experience.

You look down, you can see gum right there on the road.

It's not even a car now.

It's just a weatherproof chair out on the highway.

The only gesture of optimism left is people leaving their hands on the steering wheel.

I love that. That's hope.

Sitting there stopped, frozen solid.

But the hands on the wheel.

Like maybe the earth will just suddenly open up.

All these cars will disappear.

And I'll just take off.

And when you're in the complete dead stop you think,

"Well, at least I know it can't get any worse than this.

We aren't moving at all."

But we know in the future, traffic will get worse.

I wonder if someday it will start going backwards.

We'll be going,

(looking over shoulder backing up)

"This is some bad traffic now, boy.

This is reeally . . . bad.

Traffic so bad, you never even get where you're going.

You just have to visit whoever's house you end up at.

They go, "How was the traffic?"

You go,

"Terrible.

I don't even know who you are."

Parking Garage

The problem with the mall garage is that everything looks the same.

They try to differentiate between levels.

They put up different colors, different numbers, different letters.

What they need to do is name the levels like, "Your mother's a whore."

You would remember that.

You would go,

"I know where we're parked. We're in 'Your mother's a whore.' "

And your friend would go,

"No, we're not. We're in 'My father's an abusive alcoholic.' "

Future Outfits

I'm sick of clothes.

Sick of buying them.

Sick of picking them out of my closet.

Sick of trying to come up with different little outfits for myself every day.

I think eventually fashion won't even exist.

And we'll all just wear the same thing.

Because any time you see a movie or TV show

where there's people from the future or another planet,

they're all wearing the same outfit.

They got sick of it too.

They just decided.

"Okay everyone, listen up . . .

From now on, this is going to be the outfit for this planet . . .

We're all wearing this.

It's just a one-piece silver suit with the V-stripe and the boots.

That's it."

We should have an outfit election for Earth.

Candidates propose different looks for us.

No speeches.

Just walk out, twirl, walk off.

"That's nice. I like that one . . .

Better than the backless number.

That's not for me."

———

I think I was named best-dressed man one year.

But I don't remember the year and I don't remember what I was wearing.

I hate clothes.

I hate the selecting, the trying on, the conversing with the sales help.

There's another oxymoron, sales help.

You're either helping me or selling me but they're not the same thing.

I hate shopping bags.

I hate receipts.

I hate tags, pins, labels, hangers, buttons, zippers, drawstrings, lapels.

I hate bleach, color-safe bleach, detergents, liquids, powders, tablets, stain lifters, stain fighters, stain neutralizers, special crystals,

active ingredients, enzymes, whiteners, brighteners.

I hate hot water, cold water, warm water.

I hate getting $1 off. I hate getting ⅓ more FREE.

I hate fabric softener and static cling, so I lose either way.

I hate detergents that are good for the environment, bad for the environment, not even aware of the environment.

I hate carrying laundry bags.

I hate dry cleaning plastic, people that work at dry cleaners,

talking about my stains to the dry cleaner.

I hate and refuse to read any poster or notice anything on the wall of the dry cleaner.

If it was posted, "We reserve the right to steal your clothes,"

I wouldn't care. I'm not interested. Just take the clothes.

Just let me get the hell out of here and back to the world as soon as possible.

Maid

The first time I could afford a maid I couldn't handle the guilt.

I followed her around the whole apartment.

"I don't know why I didn't pick that stuff up.

Obviously, I could have.

I just didn't."

I'd be a terrible maid.

Because that's the attitude I'd have.

"Oh, I suppose you couldn't do this.

No, no, don't get up.

Let ME clean up YOUR filth.

Save your energy.

So you can turn this place back into a disgusting rathole after I leave.

You make me sick."

That would be me as a maid.

A Little Hair

A little hair could be a gigantic problem.

You ever have a friend staying over your house,

they use the shower.

Then later, you use the shower, and you notice

there's a little hair . . .

on the wall of the shower?

For some reason,

this little hair is the most disgusting thing you have ever encountered in your life.

And you want to get rid of it, but you don't want to touch it.

I don't know how it got up that high in the first place.

So, you've got to aim the showerhead . . . at the hair.

Sometimes the water doesn't hit it . . .

Then you have to take little handfuls of water and walk back and forth.

It's like putting out a fire in 1906.

You keep dumping them on it as it goes down the wall a foot at a time.

Sometimes the hair really hangs on.

It doesn't want to go down.

It wants to be with you.

It's a terrible relationship.

The hair loves you and you're trying to drown him.

Alone in the Bathroom

We're all alone in the bathroom.

Whatever goes wrong, you have to handle it.

Did you ever go to a big party,

go in the bathroom,

flush the toilet,

and the water starts coming . . . up?

This is the most frightening moment in the life of a human being.

You'll do anything to stop this.

You'll lose your mind and start talking to the toilet.

"No, please, don't do this to me!

Come on, you know this is not my fault.

I didn't make this happen.

Just tell me what you want . . .

I'll get you the blue thing.

The little man in the boat.

Just let me off the hook this one time . . ."

Alcatraz Faucets

What is the problem that we can't have a regular faucet in an airport bathroom?

That they will not give us a "twist-it-on, twist-it-off" human-style faucet?

Is that too risky for the general population?

Too dangerous?

"We better install the one-handed, spring-loaded, pain-in-the-ass Alcatraz-style faucets."

Those ones where you have to go,

"Hey, I got a little water there. Oo—a couple drops."

What is it that they think we would do with a faucet?

Turn them all on full?

Run out into the parking lot, laughing,

pushing each other into the bushes?

"Come on, the water's on, let's go! I turned it on full blast."

"You idiot!

We're businessmen.

We're going to miss our plane."

"Who cares? Waa-ter!"

That's how they think we'll behave.

Missed Flight

You get anxious on your way to the airport.

Because if you miss the plane, there's no alternative.

On the ground you have options.

Cars, trains, buses.

You miss your flight, there's no other forms of air travel.

The airline doesn't go,

"Well, we do have a cannon leaving in about 10 minutes."

They stamp your boarding pass, give you a helmet.

"Now, is this a direct cannon?"

"No, you will have to change cannons when you land.

And make sure you get out of the net quickly.

Because we shoot the luggage in right behind you."

They have a guy aiming it,

"Where you going, Denver?

Oh, Chicago.

(changes direction slightly)

Alright, wait a second . . ."

Horse Racing

Went to the track to see some horse racing.

I would never do that on my own.

I'm a "Go with" guy.

I really don't want to do most things.

But, I will "Go with."

Betting on horses.

So ridiculous.

Can't possibly win.

What are we betting on?

Do the horses even know that it's a race?

That's the first thing I need to be convinced of before I'm putting money down.

After the race, are the horses walking back to the stable?

"I was third."

"I was fifth."

"I was ninth."

I think they're walking back going,

(singing)

"Oat bag . . .

I get my oat bag now.

It's oat bag time for me . . ."

I mean, I'm sure the horses have some idea of what's going on.

They probably know that, "This guy on my back is in a huge hurry."

He's hitting him with the thing.

He's yelling at him, "Come on, come on!"

But the horse must get to the end and go,

(out of breath)

"We were just here!

What was the point of that?

This is where we were.

That was the longest possible route you could take to get where you wanted to be.

Why didn't we just stay here?

We would have been first . . ."

I'll tell you one thing the horses definitely do not know.

They do not know that if you should accidentally trip and break your leg at any point during the race . . .

We blow your brains out.

I have a feeling they're missing that little tidbit of information.

I think if they knew that,

you'd see some mighty careful stepping coming down that home stretch.

"Take it easy . . . take it easy . . . watch your footing . . .

You win, I'll place . . . whatever.

First or last, it's the same bag of oats, boys . . .

The important thing is your health."

Glue Factory

I have heard that when horses get old they send them to the glue factory.

I would like to know, actually, how the hell you make a horse into glue?

Who saw that potential?

Someone working in a stationery store?

Sees a horse walk by?

"You know what, I think he could be glue."

So, they have a machine with horses walking in on one side

and little glue bottles coming out the other?

That is some machine.

If you're a glue manufacturer can you look at a bunch of horses

and tell which are the really sticky ones?

"See that one, kind of weaving around?

He's out of his mind.

He'll be Krazy Glue."

Horseback

I've gone horseback riding.

Can't do it.

And they don't give you the really good horses when you're not good at it.

I found that out.

The guy says to me,

"What level rider would you say that you are?"

I said,

"I don't know. Zero. Nothing. Whatever the system is.

I can't do it.

Is that clear enough for you?

I'm going wherever the horse wants to go.

That's my 'level' . . ."

Of course after they hear that they start looking around . . .

"All right . . . is Glue Stick back yet?

How about Almost Dead?

Why don't you saddle him up?"

So I get on this U-shaped, lightning-quick steed.

I've got the only horse, you could put your feet flat on the ground while you're riding him.

"I'm riding a hammock here."

Looking up at my friends,

"I don't feel like we all got the same kind of horse here."

It is kind of a secure feeling, though.

I could walk along with him if I wanted.

And the horse wasn't too thrilled with having me either.

Because I don't know what the hell I'm doing.

So he takes control.

You know how they just stop sometimes?

And they do that slow roll of their head to look up at you?

Like, "Who the hell did I draw here . . . ?"

And they look at you with that huge black, brand-new-bowling-ball eye?

"Chill out, Hopalong. I know the trail.

I'm here every god damn day, okay?

And I really appreciate the kicking while I'm taking a leak, too.

Thanks a lot.

That really improves the already wonderful life that I have.

People either sitting on me.

Jerking my head around.

Or kicking me while I'm peeing.

It's perfect.

I'm living in a paradise here at the ranch."

Horsepower

There's just no end to the indignity of being a horse.

You go horseback riding.

The horse sees you pull up . . . in a car.

He knows, you have absolutely no real need to do this.

I get out of a car that has 500 horsepower.

So I can sit on an animal that has 1.

Why do we even use the term "horsepower"?

Is it just to further humiliate the horses?

Each Space Shuttle rocket has about 20 million horsepower.

Is there any point in continuing to compare it . . . to the horses?

Any chance of going back to using horses for rocket propulsion?

Trying to keep track of how many we're going to need?

"Hey, horse . . .

We had a rocket engine that broke down.

Can you get 20 million friends together, really fast?"

The horse has got the straw hat with the ears coming through, pulling the hayride.

"Twenty million . . . ? That's a lot . . .

I don't even have 20 friends, let alone 20 million."

Horse Trailer

To me, the toughest part of being a horse would be the trailer.

Why do they make it like that?

Is that the best way to move horses down the highway?

With their huge, fat, disgusting rear ends . . . right in my face?

Do the horses like it?

They're probably standing in the back going,

"Do you feel a draft, Bill?

I can't see anything back there, but it's awfully breezy, isn't it?

You don't think our huge, fat asses are hanging out the back of this truck, do you?

Why the hell would they do that to us?

They already sit on us and kick us while we're peeing.

Why would they drive us around with our ass sticking out of a truck, too?"

Pony

Parents deceive kids about the Pony Ride.

"It's a little horse, growing up just like you."

It's a very slow, smelly, uneventful experience.

It's not a ride.

It's a brain-dead schlep through a dusty dirt and dung patch.

I'm sitting on the thing, and the guy is leading it around a 20-foot circle.

And even as a kid I remember thinking,

"Oh, this is just too pointless.

Someone get me off this freaky little mutant."

So beyond the Pony Ride, what exactly is the contribution of the ponies to society?

Pony manure? For fertilizer?

I don't think there'll be enough of it.

Police don't use ponies for crowd control.

(looking up)

"Hey, you want to get back behind the barricade?

Little boy?

Down here . . .

I'm talking to you."

I assume that somehow somebody genetically engineered these horses to be this size.

Could they make them any size?

Could they make them the size of a quarter if they wanted?

That would be fun for Monopoly, wouldn't it?

You put him on the board . . .

"Baltic, that's one more, fine, right there, hold it right there."

Nose Job

A friend of mine is going in for a nose job next week.

Guy.

Nose job.

You know what the technical term for a nose job is?

Rhinoplasty.

RHINO.

Now, the guy is aware he has a bit of a problem.

He's obviously sensitive about it.

That's why he made the appointment.

Is it really necessary to compare him to a rhinoceros?

When you go for a hair transplant, they don't say,

"We're going to perform a Cue-ball-ectomy on you,
Mr. Johnson.

We feel the Chrome-domus has advanced

to a level we term, Skin-head-ia.

These are all medical terms, you understand."

Mad Cow

What I love about the Mad Cow Disease is we

of course attempt to blame it on the cow.

"It's not our fault, these cows are crazy.

They're nuts, they're out of their minds."

We show them sliding down these slippery ramps all out of
control.

And the cows are probably,

"Oh sure, you're drinking me, eating me, wearing me,

sneaking up on me and tipping me over, and I'm the one who's
off . . . ?"

Drugstore

Seems like it would be fun to make up these drug ingredient words.

"Now, with an extra drop of *Retsyn*."

And we all go,

"Well, that's good.

Honey, we're getting more Retsyn."

What is Retsyn?

How much were we getting?

That's medical science.

Some guy in a white coat going,

(tastes)

"Hmm . . . you know, I think it needs more Retsyn."

"How much?"

"Ah, give them an extra drop.

What the hell . . .

That should be enough.

They're lucky they're getting any Retsyn."

I had a cold a couple of weeks ago.

I go in the drugstore.

It's an entire wall of cold medications.

You ever catch yourself reading ingredients in a drugstore?

"Oh, this one has .03 tetrahydroziline.

That's a good amount of that."

Sometimes you have to contemplate some existential questions.

"All right, so this product is quick acting . . .

But this one is long lasting.

So, when do I need to feel good?

Now?

Or later?

I don't know."

I like how they always show you how the medicine works on TV.

Where the guy says,

"Here's the human body."

It's always this guy.

(Arms wide. Palms facing out. Head to the side.)

You know this guy.

No face.

Mouth open.

This is how drug companies see the public.

He's always got the tube coming down here and then there's the circle.

(Throat. Stomach.)

These are the complex inner workings of the human body, I assume.

I'm sure when you go to medical school, they probably put that up on the board the first day.

"Okay everyone, now remember, you got your tube coming down from the mouth.

And that goes into your circle area.

That's pretty much all we know.

That's it for today.

Don't miss tomorrow.

We're going to practice making people wait in a little room in their underwear . . .

And then you will all be doctors.

That's all there is to it."

Then in the commercial, they have to show you the pain.

That's the part where they say,

"Here's where you hurt."

Pain is usually represented by some sort of lightning attacking the guy.

Glowing redness is popular.

Sometimes parts of the guy's body will just burst into flames.

Sometimes the whole guy is out of focus.

I've never had a doctor say to me,

"Are you having any pain?"

"Yes, I am."

"Are you having any lightning with the pain?"

"Tiny hammers banging on you?"

"Have you seemed to be in a fun-house mirror at any time?"

Then they tell you about the pain-relieving ingredient.

There always has to be a lot of that.

Nobody wants any amount less than "EXTRA-STRENGTH."

"EXTRA-STRENGTH" is actually the absolute minimum we will accept at this point.

You can't even get "STRENGTH."

"STRENGTH" is not available.

They don't even make "STRENGTH" anymore.

Some people are not satisfied with "EXTRA."

They want "MAXIMUM."

"I want 'MAXIMUM-STRENGTH.'

I am in a tremendous amount of pain.

Give me . . . the MAXIMUM ALLOWABLE HUMAN DOSAGE.

Figure out what will kill me and then back it off a little bit."

Doctor's Waiting Room

There's that little bit of arrogance in the medical community

that I think we could all live without.

Like, when you go to see the doctor, they don't just let you see
the doctor.

You must first wait in the waiting room.

There's no chance of not waiting.

That's the name of the room.

Just the fact that doctors have Waiting Rooms is like saying,

"All appointments are meaningless.

My schedule is bogus."

You sit there, you pretend you're reading your little magazine,

you're actually looking at the other people . . .

(to oneself)

"I wonder what he's got . . .

that guy's a goner."

Then they call you.

You look around at the other people,

(very pleased)

"Well, I guess I've been chosen . . ."

And you get very excited,

because you think you're going to see the doctor.

But you're not.

You're just going into the next, smaller Waiting Room.

Now, you don't even have your magazine.

Now you've got your pants around your ankles,

you're sitting on that butcher paper they pull out over the table.

Sometimes I bring a pickle with me.

Put it next to me right there on the table.

In case the doctor wants to wrap the whole thing up for a to-go order.

But medically speaking, it's always good to be in a small room.

You don't want to be in a large room,

like those operating theaters that they have with stadium seating.

You don't want them doing anything to you that makes other doctors go,

"Well, I have to see this. Are you kidding? Are they really going to do that?

Are there seats? Can we get in?"

———

Doctors always want your pants off.

"Get your pants off and get in there and then I will tell you what I think."

"The doctor would like to see you with no pants. Just get them off."

It really gives him an advantage.

In any difference of opinion,

Pants always beats No Pants.

But I hate the extra wait, so I start screwing around with some of his stuff.

"Maybe I'll turn that thing up a little bit. Whatever the hell that does."

Take all the tongue depressors out, lick them all, put them all back in.

Two can play at this waiting game.

Just once I would like to say to the doctor,

"You know what? I'm not ready for you yet.

Why don't you go back in your little office.

I'll be in in a minute.

And get your pants off."

Why does a doctor need that little office anyway?

I guess he doesn't want people to see him looking stuff up—

"What the hell was that?"

(quickly paging through a book)

"Jesus Christ.

That was kind of gross.

That wasn't the tube or the circle."

May Contain

I like when ingredients say,

"May contain one or more of the following."

"May contain"?

What if it's important?

What if you have diabetes?

"Does it have sugar?"

"Maybe . . .

We're not saying.

Why don't you just eat it?

Then we'll all know for sure."

Chock Full o'Nuts

Why does coffee always come from these made-up places like Arabica?

Where is that?

Near Jamoca Almond Fudge?

Coffee always has fake names.

"Chock Full o'Nuts."

How many more years does this go on before someone says to them, "Excuse me. What are you talking about? What nuts?"

The head of the company probably went,

"You can call it Pocket Full of Balls, as far as I'm concerned.

It's coffee. No one cares."

Improved Tide

I was in the supermarket the other day and I see Tide has been improved.

Do they sense that people are out there,

"How was your wash?"

"I don't know . . . It was alright . . . I guess.

Could've been better."

I have no idea how they improved it.

They're always showing you how detergents get out *bloodstains*.

Kind of a violent image, isn't it?

I think if you have a T-shirt with bloodstains all over it,

maybe laundry isn't your biggest problem right now.

Maybe get rid of the body before you do the wash?

Who are they appealing to?

Somehow I don't picture Charles Manson

standing over the machine with that little cup of fabric softener.

Chopsticks

I'll tell you what I like about Chinese people.

They're really hanging in there with the chopsticks.

Obviously, they've seen the fork . . .

But they're,

"Yes, very nice.

But we're staying with the sticks."

I don't know how they missed it.

Chinese farmers working in the field with a shovel all day.

Shovel . . . spoon . . . come on.

There it is.

You're not plowing 40 acres with a couple of pool cues.

Cannibalism

One of the most powerful things in the world is hunger.

Hunger will make people do amazing things.

The proof of that is cannibalism.

That's hungry.

Cannibalism actually exists.

How do they live?

They're eating. What do they say?

"This is good.

Who is this?"

I would think the hardest part of being a cannibal is getting a good night's sleep.

Constantly waking up in the middle of the night,

"Who is it?

Who's there?

What do you want?

You look hungry.

Are you hungry?

You get the hell out of here right now."

People Owner's Manual

See, each man and each woman actually does have an owner's manual.

Nothing's written down anywhere.

But the directions for operation of an individual in a relationship are detailed and specific nonetheless.

So when you start out with someone, you're essentially driving a strange car for the first time.

But none of the controls are labeled.

So, the wipers can come on at strange times.

Sometimes you stall.

We've all met people with bad steering, no brakes, needs a muffler.

Headlights a little dim, too much in the trunk, not enough under the hood.

Prone to backfiring, won't turn over, and just plain out of gas.

Which is why when people get ready to get married

they so often seem to choose basic transportation.

It's simple, it's reliable, and it gets you there.

That's important on a long trip.

Favor

There's two kinds of favors.

Big favor.

Small favor.

You can measure the size of the favor

by the size of the pause the person takes after they ask,

"Could you do me a favor?"

No pause, small favor.

"Could you do me a favor and hand me that pencil?"

But if it's,

"Could you do me a favor . . . ?

What I need is . . ."

The longer it takes them to say it, the bigger the pain it's going to be.

Also the human is the only species that does favors.

Animals don't do favors.

A lizard doesn't say to a cockroach,

"Could you do me a favor and hold still for a second, I'd like to eat you alive."

That, by the way, would be a big favor.

That cockroach is really putting himself out.

Men's Attention

Why are women always trying to draw men's attention

to every area of your body we're already totally focused on?

Short skirts, push-up bra.

Do we really need the coaching?

I find some of these sexy outfits women wear a little insulting.

It's like they feel we need a highlighter.

Don't tell me where to look.

If we can't handle the leering and gawking by now . . .

I don't know why we even bother setting up all these construction sites.

You know women walking by construction sites is what built this country.

There's no other way to get people to do these jobs.

Women complain but this system is working.

"If you guys want to stand on the street,

and be obnoxious all day,

you're going to have to at least pretend to be building a building."

Beauty Contest

Men can justify anything to look at women.

"What about a swimsuit competition?"

"Yes, women in swimsuits competing.

That makes perfect sense."

The whole concept of the beauty contest itself.

Think about that.

"You are very attractive.

I challenge you."

Pocketbooks

Women have different ways of adjusting men's proximity.

The pocketbook is probably their main distance controlling unit.

All the equipment in there is designed to keep men within a certain optimal range.

If the men are too far away, they're like,

"Too far.

More makeup, eye colors, perfumes, bring them in."

But if they get too close it's,

"Oh, too close—

Mace, rape whistles, keys between the fingers.

Back up, dude."

Flower Power

Probably the only thing that enables a man to keep a relationship going over a long period of time

is the existence of flowers.

A man alone cannot survive in a relationship.

But a man with some flowers has a chance.

If there were no flowers on earth,

the world would be men and lesbians, that's it.

And that's why flower stores are not set up right for what men need.

It should be that you walk in, you tell them what you did wrong,

they give you the flowers for that,

and you just continue right out the back.

The "Alright, Your Brother's Not an Idiot" bouquet.

The "Your Career's Important Too" basket.

Also, any man carrying a big bouquet of flowers

is the king of that street.

No other man with a woman wants to be seen anywhere near this guy.

Or he gets, (elbow jab)

"See? That's what I'm talking about . . ."

Because he's carrying flowers.

He could have a severed head in the other hand.

She doesn't notice that.

Always Friends

There are certain friends in your life who are always your friends.

You don't call them, they call you.

You don't call back, they call again.

You're late, they wait.

You don't show up, they're not upset.

You try and stab them, they understand.

Thin, Single, and Neat

I am not gay.

I am however, thin, single, and neat.

Sometimes when someone is thin, single, and neat,

people assume they are gay because that is the stereotype.

You normally don't think of gay people as fat, sloppy, and married.

Although I'm sure some are—I don't want to perpetuate a stereotype.

But they're probably in the minority in the gay community.

And probably discriminated against because of that.

People say to them,

"You know, Joe, I enjoy being gay with you,

but I think it's about time you got in shape, tucked your shirt in and lost the wife."

Baby Visit

My friend just had a baby.

Lot of pressure to see this baby.

"You have got to see the baby.

When are you coming over to see the baby?

See the baby. See the baby."

Nobody ever wants you to come over and see their grandfather.

"You gotta see him. He's sooo cute. A hundred and sixty-eight pounds, four ounces.

I love when they're this age.

He's a thousand months.

He went to the bathroom by himself today."

Just once I would like to meet a couple that goes,

"You know, we're not that happy with the baby,

I think we really made a big mistake.

We should've gotten an aquarium."

Those baby visits can get a lit-tle boring.

You have to yawn.

I don't think there's anything wrong with yawning.

I hate when people try not to yawn.

Teeth clenched, their cheeks start vibrating, trying to keep their mouth closed.

It's like watching someone get electrocuted.

Night Guy/Morning Guy

I think the secret to our great American economy is relentless, annoying advertising. And our natural dumbness.

That just works so well together.

I saw a Mattress Store commercial,

"No Payments 'til June."

Because they know we're going to go,

"Oh . . . June . . . pfff

Well, that's not really my problem then, is it?

Besides, it'll probably never be June.

And if it ever is, that's June Guy's problem.

So what if I'm broke in the present?

I'm sure June Guy will have gotten some money somehow.

And wouldn't June Guy want me to be enjoying my life now?"

———

We do the same thing when we're watching TV late at night.

"What about work tomorrow?

You've got to get up.

You've got a big day."

"Oh, that's Morning Guy's problem.

I'm night guy.

I don't worry about that stuff.

I party.

I rock the house.

Fire up the next episode and crack open a new sleeve of Oreos for me and my Merry Men!

I'm Night Guy."

Then, morning comes . . .

Alarm goes off.

You're totally trashed.

Crumbs in the bed.

"Oohh . . . Why did I do that?

I hate you, Night Guy."

Night Guy always screws Morning Guy.

He becomes,

Coffee All Day Guy.

Who turns into,

Can't Sleep at Night Guy.

And then into,

Doesn't Do His Work Guy.

Who becomes

Out of a Job Guy.

You think Night Guy cares?

No.

He's sleeping on a brand-new mattress

courtesy of

No Payments 'til June Guy.

The
Double O's

For about two years after I finished the series I didn't do anything.

I moved my life back to New York.

I had breakfast with Colin Quinn everyday.

I played pool at Amsterdam Billiards at night. Very late sometimes.

I met and married my wonderful wife, Jessica.

But no stand-up.

No writing. Nothing.

Felt lost. And wanted to.

———

My friend Chris Misiano, the same guy whose brother told us about comedy clubs in New York thirty years earlier, and I decided it would be a good time

to drive from NY to LA in a convertible with the top down the whole way no matter what the weather.

We chose one of the greatest convertibles of all time,

the '89 Porsche 911 Speedster, and did the trip.

Eight days.

Bought a meteorite in New Mexico.

In LA, two of my comedy pals, Chris Rock and Mario Joyner, were doing a show

at the Universal Amphitheater and I went to see them.

The amphitheater is a big house, about six thousand seats.

I sat there watching these two smooth, confident professionals handle that room

and that crowd so easily.

I laughed and enjoyed that show so much.

And then I thought,

"What an amazing talent and skill set that is to witness.

What a great time we're having in this audience.

How are they able to do that?!"

I know, I know it sounds so dumb that I would think that.

But we all are dumb from time to time.

Then I thought,

"I want to do that. I want to be like them."

Then, "Wait a minute! That's what I used to be!

I used to know how to do everything they are doing.

I still want to be that."

―――

This has happened to me over and over again in my life.

You get so used to doing what you do, you don't see what it is anymore.

I still see stand-up comedians and think,

"How in the world can they do that?"

Getting out of your head is one of the most important places to visit.

I do not get upset with myself when I am dumb.

Because the essential building blocks of comedy, very often,

are an elegant intertwining of really dumb and really smart.

You need both to make comedy.

To pick a random example,

the bit about my daughter leaving home for college is like

having a baby alligator in your bathtub for too long and then realizing,

"You know, I think we got to get this thing the hell out of here."

Making the analogy is the smart part.

But you also need the dumbness of a person leaving an alligator in their bathtub

for an extended period of time to make the joke work.

It's actually a big part of what you're laughing at.

A moron with an alligator that doesn't realize what's going on.

―――

Anyway, I go to the Chris Rock show.

I realize I want my skill set back.

I want to be a stand-up comedian.

Again.

One problem.

I got no act.

A few months after the series ended I did a stand-up special for HBO

that I'd owed them for a few years.

I decided to call it *I'm Telling You for the Last Time*, and I would retire my whole set

that I had spent years working on.

Smart, right? And dumb.

So there I was, quite a popular fellow at the time.

Audiences would definitely buy tickets to see me.

But . . . nothing to say when I get onstage.

―――

Back again to me and Chris Rock.

We're having dinner at an Italian restaurant in Manhattan.

I explain my situation.

Chris says, "Well, at least you know there's only one way to do it."

It did feel great to be reminded of that.

I didn't have to waste one second of time wondering how to approach the problem.

I don't use writers.

So, it's back to tiny clubs with flimsy stuff, night after night, month after month.

And it takes however long it takes.

When you see a comedian with a ton of great stuff, what you're really marveling at,

or should be, is

"How could someone crawl on their belly that great a distance?"

So, here's my belly crawl of these ten years.

Doing Nothing

A lot of people ask me,

"Hey, Jerry, so what do you do now?

You don't have a show anymore.

What do you do?"

I'll tell you what I do.

. . . Nothing.

And I know you're thinking,

"Hey, that sounds pretty good.

I might like to do nothing myself."

But doing nothing is not as easy as it looks.

You can get pretty busy doing nothing.

Because when you're doing nothing, you're actually free to do anything.

Which can easily lead to doing something.

Which cuts into my nothing,

and forces me to have to drop everything.

Weddings

I've been Best Man twice at weddings.

Always thought it was a bit much.

Seems like it should be a groom, and a pretty good man . . .

Really tries.

I mean, if *I'm* the Best Man, why is she marrying him?

_____

But I do stand before you tonight as a very happily married man.

So, I can recommend being married to you.

I cannot, however, recommend getting married.

Because of the Wedding.

The bride of course is the engine that drives the wedding.

The bride is into it.

The bride reads *Bride* magazine.

Which is the thickest, heaviest, most frightening magazine on the planet.

It lands hard on the coffee table.

"BANG!"

"What was that?!"

"That . . . was *Bride* magazine."

———

Bride magazine causes the bride to get Bride Brain.

The Bridal Brain is a world of infinite possibilities.

Ideas like,

"Honey, I think I'm going to need 20 more feet of dress that just drags off the end of my dress.

Because I'm the god damned bride, that's why.

I dragged him to the altar,

I may as well drag this too."

———

Bride Pride is real.

And Bride Pride is justified.

A woman absolutely deserves wide public recognition that,

"I got one of these clowns to act right."

Mind you, a bride is also a very keyed up individual.

You never want to surprise a bride.

You never want to make a sudden change in the bridal environment.

Because a bride can snap like that.

And they always do.

And that's really the best part of the wedding.

When the bride goes berserk.

And rips some hapless wedding worker a new one

because somebody screwed up

on the "Castle of Shrimp."

"Where is the cocktail sauce in the moat surrounding the castle?!

Where are the lobster claws guarding the gate?!

Do you know how embarrassing this is for me?!

I am mortified.

(rips arm away)

LET GO OF ME . . .

No, I—will—not—lower—my—voice.

Because This Is My Special Day, that's why.

And you tell that band's leader I want 'Colour My World'

and 'Wind Beneath My Wings,'

or I will shove that mic stand so far up his . . .

Oh, we're taking more pictures? Yes, of course.

Come, children, carry my dragging ego.

We're going down to the simulated duck pond to further document my beauty."

Because there must be a wedding album after the wedding.

The purpose of which is to equal the weight and intense boredom

of the *Bride* magazine that started the whole thing.

———

I had to wear the tuxedo, which, I am convinced, was invented by a woman.

"Well, they're all the same, we might as well dress them all the same."

To me, a wedding is the joining together of a beautiful, glowing bride

. . . and some guy.

The tuxedo also functions as a Wedding Safety Device for the bride.

In case the groom chickens out,

everybody just takes one step over and the ceremony continues.

That's why they don't say,

"Do you take Bob Johnson to be your lawfully wedded husband?"

They say,

"Do you take THIS man?"

Whoever's standing there . . .

———

The tuxedo is also the Universal Male Symbol for somebody trying to pull a fast one.

Think of where you see the tuxedo . . .

The groom wears it to project an image of sophisticated refinement.

He is hoping nobody at the wedding will notice

the head popping out of the top of the suit

belongs to the same degenerate, ill-mannered ignoramus

everyone there has known for years.

It doesn't work.

He knew that it wouldn't.

And that's why it's just rented.

The tuxedo is the world's most rented clothing.

Needed only for quick scams and flimflams.

Award shows, casinos, limos, proms, and strip clubs.

"I just need to fool a small group of people for a short period of time.

I'll bring it right back."

Even a Halloween costume is purchased outright and kept with pride.

A 10-year-old child makes a stronger commitment to being a skeleton

than a grown man to being a dignified, mature adult.

And,

I'm sure there are couples here tonight planning

Some kind of huge blow-out wedding.

Do not applaud.

Do not cheer.

Do not go, "woo."

Do not acknowledge me in any way.

Just sit quietly in the dark . . .

Because there is something about this wedding I need to tell you.

Something your family will not tell you.

Your friends will not tell you.

Only I, your strange little TV friend . . .

I might be the only person you know

that can tell you the complete, straight up, honest truth.

Which is this:

Nobody wants to go to your wedding.

We're not looking forward to it.

We are not excited, like you are.

Most of us are getting these invitations and throwing it on the ground,

"Oh Jesus Christ . . . it's on a SATURDAY . . ."

Now I don't want you to get the wrong impression.

I don't want you to think we're not happy for you, because we are.

We all think it's "great."

You two have met.

You want to be together.

You want to go off and do whatever you want to do in life.

Just do it.

Why is it necessary to ruin the day of 150 other people?

Who are not actually part of this.

Can't you leave us alone . . . ?

They cannot.

They will not leave us alone.

Couples are always agonizing over these guest lists.

"Oh, we *have* to invite them, they would be so upset."

No, they won't.

They'll be clicking their heels.

Because it's a bad party.

Bad music.

Bad food.

Everyone here has been to a good party.

You know what a good party is like . . .

If you were going to plan a good party,

would you first invite all the oldest people you know?

So you can sit there watching them eat?

In that disgusting way that they do?

Why do old people eat so badly?

They have the most experience at it.

What age is it when you can no longer feel

That you have a piece of food on your face?

Do these nerve endings just die out at 75?

You're trying to have a conversation . . .

You can't do it.

"Don't you feel that right there . . . ?

You got a piece of rice . . .

It's just hanging from your lip.

It's a very distinct pinpoint sensation.

Why do you not perceive it?"

They breathe out, it swings out.

They inhale, it swings back.

———

I don't need to see people dance that have not otherwise moved in the past 5 years.

Going into these hazy *Soul Train* memory convulsion flashbacks.

"I guess I'll just fire off some major muscle groups in a random order . . .

I can't remember . . . what I used to do."

———

The best part of the wedding, from the male perspective,

is it's the only possible situation where

you're essentially gathering this woman's entire family together and announcing to them,

"I am now going to have sex with your daughter.

We're going to go to a hotel somewhere right after this and I'm going to do everything I can think of."

And everyone applauds.

Her father's vigorously shaking your hand.

"Well done, young man."

Then about halfway through the reception,

the Bride and Groom themselves actually realize how bad it is and just leave in the middle.

They come downstairs.

They've changed.

They've packed.

"Well, this sucks. We'll see you later . . .

We're going to Barbados to have sex.

You enjoy the dry cake and our relatives . . ."

And they leave you sitting there.

That's why everyone follows them out the door,

"Give me a handful of that rice."

And the old people go,

(taking it from his lip and throwing it)

"Here's mine, too."

Divorce

And I'm sure there's women here going,

"I know you think you're very funny, Jerry, but marriage is a pretty big change

in a person's life. And it's important that everyone is there."

Divorce is a big change.

How come I don't have to go to that?

And I would go to that.

At least I'm at a party for something that's going to last.

It's rare that you hear about a divorce that didn't work out.

"Yeah, it turned out that Jim's asshole qualities and Sue's bitchiness were just temporary.

They were delightful, lovely people that should never have gotten divorced in the first place."

Live Together

I was never much for the "live with" relationship approach.

"Let's see . . ."

There's nothing to see.

You're going to see what you've been seeing.

Besides, living with a woman who wants to get married.

That's like living with a murderer in the house.

Can't relax. Can't sleep.

Keep waking up in the middle of the night.

"I think I heard something downstairs."

"What was it?"

"I don't know, sounded like a caterer setting up."

Commitment/Rejection

One of the nice things about getting married,

besides making the commitment to the person you want
to be with, is the rejection of a lot of people you don't want to
be with.

That means a lot to me too.

Marriage is a sacred bond, yes.

But it's also a nice way to tell a lot of people to get lost.

I feel it should be part of the ceremony.

"Do you take this woman . . . as opposed to some of these
other losers I see sitting here."

———

You can really get sick of yourself when you're single.

And I was single for a long time.

You get so tired of hearing yourself say the same things over
and over again.

"Would you like to come up to my apartment for a glass of
wine?"

Oh, just shut the hell up already.

Nobody wants any more wine from you.

Stop offering people wine.

Haven't you served people enough wine . . . ?

Marriage Chess

It's all about listening.

A lot of wives complain

that their husbands do not listen . . .

I've never heard my wife say this . . . she may have . . .

I don't know.

———

But here's what I do know.

Ladies, your husband wants to make you happy.

He's working on it.

He's planning it.

And he's thinking about it every second.

But he *cannot* do it.

Sometimes we do it.

We don't know how we did it.

We can't ask,

"What did I do?"

That looks like you don't know what you're doing.

Can't do nothing.

Woman says,

"I can't believe you're doing this."

Man says,

"Doing what?"

Woman starts crying.

Man says,

"I didn't do anything."

Woman says,

"Exactly."

So, it's a bit of a chess game . . .

Except the board is flowing water,

and all the chess pieces

are made of . . . smoke.

You can make all the moves you want,

it will not affect the outcome of the game.

Married/Single

The other problem I have being married,

is I can no longer pretend to be interested in the dating problems of my single friends.

"You called some girl, she didn't call you back . . .

I don't care."

"Can't seem to meet the right person?

Change your entire personality."

———

When I was single I had married friends.

I would not visit their homes.

I found their lives to be pathetic and depressing.

Now that I'm married, I have no single friends.

I find their lives to be meaningless and trivial experiences.

In both cases, I believe I was correct.

Whichever side of marriage you're on

You don't get what the other people are doing.

I can't hang out with single guys.

If you don't have a wife, we have nothing to talk about.

You have a girlfriend?

That's Wiffle ball, my friend.

You're playing Paintball War.

I'm in Afghanistan with real loaded weapons.

Married guys play with full clips and live rounds.

"This is not a drill."

Single guy is sitting on a merry-go-round, blowing on a pinwheel.

I'm driving a truckful of nitro down a dirt road.

You single guys here tonight, looking at me . . .

"Hey, Jerry, what if I want to be a married guy like you?

What do I got to have if I want to be a married guy?"

I'll tell you what you got to have.

You better have some answers, buddy . . .

You better have some answers for that woman.

Women have a lot of questions.

Their brains are strong.

Active.

And on high alert at all times.

You're sleeping, she's researching.

(flipping book pages quickly)

———

The female brain is cooking all the time.

The female brain is one of the most competent and capable organs in all of the biological universe.

Girl Power.

There is nothing the female brain cannot do.

It will solve all problems of Earth and Life.

Having done that,

it will move on to the hypothetical.

Theoretical situations.

That may or *may not* occur.

The female needs to know

How you MIGHT respond.

"If you faked your own death,

and I found out about it,

what would you say THEN . . . ?"

"What are we talking about now?"

"Oh, I dreamt the whole thing last night, so don't deny it!"

———

Being married is like being on a game show

And you're always in the Lightning Round.

I have a game show podium.

Set up in my living room.

I wake up in the morning.

Stand behind the podium.

Try and answer all my wife's questions.

And get on with the god damn day.

I've got a little hand button clicker.

"I'll take movies I think we saw together for $200."

My wife, of course, is the returning champion from last week.

"I'll take details of a 10-minute conversation

we had at three o'clock in the morning, eight years ago,

and I'd like to bet everything I have on that, Alex.

I'm going for the win right here . . ."

The husband, of course, doesn't have a clue.

"I'm sorry, sir.

You did not win the weekend sex package

or the guilt-free televised sporting event."

Thank you for playing

Are You Even Listening to Me?

And don't forget to take that big bag of garbage with you

On your way out of the studio . . ."

A Wife Is an Extra Head

A wife is not a relationship.

A wife is an extra head mounted next to your head.

I also have kid heads.

I have a dog head.

I have a parakeet head.

And whenever I want to go somewhere all these heads start talking to each other.

"I want to go here.

I want to go there.

Where do you think you're going?

Woof, woof,

tweet, tweet."

Tone

One of the things I did not know when I was single

that I found out after I got married,

is that every single day of my married life

I would be discussing

the tone in my voice.

I was not aware, how often I speak, in the

incorrect tone.

I thought it was a marriage.

Apparently, it's a musical.

I walk around the house now with one of those

round black glee club things,

"Hmmmm . . . how about that one?

(angrier)

Hmmmmm . . . am I getting *closer*?!"

"It's your tone."

"My what?"

"Your tone."

"My tone?"

"Yes, your tone."

"What's wrong with my tone?"

"I don't like your tone."

"What do you want me to do?"

"You better change your tone.

Figure out what tone you're in

and get into another tone."

And women are correct.

As they always are.

The Male Tone does change over the course of the relationship.

In the beginning, as the male pursues the female,

we raise our voice two full octaves.

(higher voice)

We talk like this.

"Because Chinese food or Italian sounds great.

Maybe we could take a drive or go for a walk . . . ?"

My actual speaking voice

that I am using right now

to communicate with you

is NOT WELCOME in my house.

That's why I'm out here talking to you . . .

If I walked in my own house . . .

Which I paid for, by the way.

Not relevant.

I just wanted to mention it . . .

And I was to say,

"I HAVE GOT TO GET SOMETHING TO EAT."

If I said it like that . . .

First of all, any guy I know would say,

"Eat whatever you want.

I don't care what you eat . . ."

Any woman will say,

"Why are you yelling at me?!"

"I'm not yelling.

I'm just hungry . . ."

And then the fight breaks out.

And when the fight breaks out, now you're whitewater kayaking.

You've got a plastic helmet on,

you're going down.

You're popping up.

You're catching foam.

Just keep paddling.

It will eventually calm down.

And this is when the woman's tone of voice changes.

Yes, the women are included in this too.

All women, when they get in the fight with the man,

must at some point in the argument imitate the voice of the man.

And women, in that beautifully organized way that they have,

have somehow all arranged to do the exact same impression.

"Oh, you always say I never said I would definitely go, you said, I might go, not definitely, you say you're not comfortable with my friends, when we go with your friends,

and my friends and your friends . . ."

Who the hell is this guy?

I have never heard anyone talk like this.

(woman imitating man)

"You should hear how you sound.

If you could hear yourself . . ."

I hear myself.

My mouth is here, my ear is here.

I can hear it perfectly.

Relationship Underwear

Men want the same thing from our underwear that we want from the women in our lives.

A certain amount of support.

And a certain amount of freedom.

I want the loose attitude and cool breezes of boxer-short living.

But I also need a woman that's got some tight cotton and strong elastic, like a brief.

So, I know I've got a real home.

Where I feel centered,

knowing which way I'm pointed in this world.

Blind Sight

I think the blind man gets the best women.

Because in choosing a woman, sight is the ultimate handicap.

The fashions,

the makeup,

the hair color,

the streaks,

the highlights,

the sparkles.

A sighted man can't see straight.

Blind man sees through all of it.

You better make some sense when you're talking to a blind man.

Or else he's like,

"Honey, you could be wearing the hottest outfit in the world.

But these things you're saying,

you're useless."

Blindness is THE handicap to have in dating.

Deafness, I think, would definitely come in handy later when you're married.

Then when the kids come along,

paralyzed.

"I would love to go to your soccer game.

I have to sit here and watch football on TV."

———

Blindness improves every phase of the relationship.

He doesn't have to deal with his woman saying things like,

"Are you even listening to me?"

"Of course, I'm listening.

What the hell else do you think I'm doing?"

"I swear sometimes when I talk, it's like you're just staring off in space."

"Well . . . I'm not."

Lip Liner

The things people do to make themselves more attractive.

Like the women that do the lip liner like it's a dead body at a crime scene.

I would like to say to all women on behalf of the men of planet Earth, "We see your lips."

You want to highlight with a little color, fine.

You don't need to put a ground marker.

We're not parachuting in.

It's "out of bounds lipstick."

You can't go outside the lines, ladies, we've got to have some kind of rules.

Stay within the lines.

Do not draw in features wherever you wish you had them on your face.

This is not Toontown, we're human beings.

No Important Calls

I just don't know why people always panic when their cell phone rings.

They always seem to think it's an important call.

"Oh my god, is that my phone?

Is that your phone?

Whose phone is that?

Is that my ring?

Is that 'Funky Town'?

'Got to make a move to a town that's right for me . . .'

That *is* my phone."

Such urgency.

When are we all going to realize?

There are no important calls.

Here's how you know it's not important.

The call is coming from someone you know.

And they're calling you.

Do you know any important people?

I don't.

I know a lot of people that think they're important.

Don't want to talk to them . . .

What two things do you say after every telephone call of your life?

"Who was that?"

"Nobody."

"What did they want?"

"Nothing."

*69

We live in a new phone world now.

Nothing innocent about a telephone anymore.

We live in a *69, caller ID, caller ID block, kind of world.

"Who's calling me, trying to get to me, without me knowing that it's them?

I should be calling them, without them knowing it's me.

That would give me an advantage over them."

That's a lot of suspicion.

Remember when the phone would ring and someone would say,

(singsong voice)

"I'll . . . get . . . it . . ."

You don't hear that anymore.

———

Now the phone rings,

"NOBODY MOVE . . .

Who the hell is 5-1-3?

It better not be who I think it is . . . !"

———

*69 was the first phone feature they came out with that

I thought was a little hostile to the calling party.

Someone calls.

They hang up.

You hit that *69.

"Nice try, creep. Oh, I know all about your little call . . ."

———

And 69?

That's the number they pick for this thing?

So that means there isn't one person at the phone company that went to junior high school?

How did that slip through an entire organization?

If you worked at the phone company,

and you heard they were doing this . . .

wouldn't you walk into that meeting and go,

"69?

Are you guys kidding me . . . ?!

That's the number you guys came up with for the new feature?

What the hell is going on in here?"

"We're the phone company.

We can pick any number we want.

68.

70.

I can't wait to hear what you got for 3-Way Calling."

BlackBerry Relation-Chips

My wife is on the BlackBerry now.

These people have totally left the conscious world.

They walk around with it in their hand because that is what BlackBerry commands them to do.

And they're always comparing you to what's on the BlackBerry.

"Uh-huh, which is really more interesting here?"

Is there anything worse than when they do that slow head drop?

And they just leave you.

What am I supposed to do?

Just look for planes now?

Do we even know what rudeness is anymore?

What if I held a magazine up in front of your face and just read it while you're talking?

Is that impolite in any way?

My wife's BlackBerry keeps advancing on me.

It started in the car.

Then she brought it into the house.

The other night I found it in the bed.

It was on the other pillow just blinking at me.

Like,

"You're not part of what she and I have."

I tried to smother it with another pillow but it doesn't use oxygen.

A couple of days later, my wife found it in the bottom of a bowl of yogurt.

"Oh, it said BlackBerry, I guess I got confused."

≈ Links

I need to meet some new people.

Different people.

People that are not like the people I know now.

I don't care if they're smart or funny or interesting or nice

as long as they don't send links in emails.

That's the kind of people I feel very drawn to right now.

"Did you get the link?

I sent you a link.

Did you see the link?"

"Yeah, I got the link.

Your link is not my only link.

Got a lot of links.

Get in the Link Line.

I will get to your link."

3 days later . . .

"I tried to open it. The link wouldn't open."

"Okay. Here's what I'm going to do. I'm going to resend the link."

"No. No. Do not.

Don't resend it.

I didn't want it the first time."

It's 8 messages back and forth to see a video of a fat guy tripping over a cat.

"Did you see it? What did you think?"

"I just sent you a link to a video of me blowing my brains out if this is what life is now.

Open that.

That's the last link."

Facebook

Of course Facebook,

another great trash receptacle of human time . . .

Which everyone loves because not only

does the name Facebook complete the final whoring out of the word "book."

I'm sure looking at pictures of Timmy and Tammy drunk in Cabo

is the same as reading *Moby-Dick*.

But also because it expresses the outlook of young, dumb people, which is so beautiful.

That, "People are so great."

And, "It's great to connect with people."

I am hoping that I live long enough to see these young people in their 50s.

Because when you blow out the candles on that 50th birthday cake

your first thought is going to be,

"The fewer people I have anything to do with, the better off I'm going to be."

Connecting with people is why there are lawyers, mace and cease-and-desist orders.

Because of two people that "connected" with each other.

Twitter

And of course, Twitter.

Tweeting, of course, was originally invented by birds in trees.

"Phoo-weet Phoo-weet,"

that was the first Tweet.

It meant "sex, worms, sex, worms."

Hashtag, #rocksmyworld

As humans we were so impressed with this form of communication we decided,

"Why should birds be the only ones

dropping an annoying series of small daily turds upon the earth?

We can do it too."

Preferency People

I do not like to have coffee with the "Preferency People."

Who have very strong preferences, about what they prefer.

Like whichever artificial sweetener . . .

"I like the Blue."

"I need the Pink."

"Excuse me, do you have the Yellow?"

Because there's such a huge difference

between Powdered Aluminum Sweet and Cancer

And Great-Grandchildren Birth Defect Potassium Palmitate.

One's got an aftertaste.

I love that meltdown.

"Oh my god, there was a taste

and then there was another taste that came after that taste.

Then 20 minutes later in the car.

I burped, and there was a third taste."

Repeat Story

I guess it's all the tech stuff.

But don't people seem a little hazy now all the time?

A little fuzzy.

They start talking.

Then they go,

"Was I talking to you about this?

Were you there with me . . . ?

You were there. Was that you?

Did I know you then . . . ?

Is this your story that you originally told to me?

So, we did talk.

I wasn't there.

You were. I didn't know.

We hadn't met.

And I thought I was you.

Let's talk again soon . . ."

———

But a lot of times people will launch into a story they have already told you.

And you go,

"Well, I guess I'm going on this ride again."

Now you're in your own little one-act play.

Trying to re-create all the same responses you had the first time.

Intrigued.

Surprised.

Sad.

Outraged.

Supportive.

And now you're terrified they're going to catch you.

"Wait, I did tell you this.

Why didn't you stop me?"

"Because I'm focusing on my performance."

The two of you end up just staring at each other.

Realizing, one's a liar.

The other's a bore.

The whole relationship's a fraud.

Blowing Smoke

Whenever someone gives you a compliment now, for some reason they have to follow it with,

"And I'm not just blowing smoke up your ass."

Why are we even in that area?

So, you feel good for 5 seconds

and then you have this image of asses and smoke going up . . .

Who did this even happen to, that we started saying it?

(walking with legs squeezed tightly together)

"That was a lovely gesture that young man made.

I certainly wasn't expecting him to do that . . ."

―――

I remember a time when people used to kiss ass.

They used to kiss up.

Kiss ass.

They used to say,

"He's a real ass kisser."

I guess the kissing's not getting it done anymore.

"You better blow some smoke up there, buddy . . ."

―――

Similarly,

whenever someone has a great number of a certain item,

you will often hear them say,

"Well, I have those coming OUT of my ass."

"Really?"

"Yes.

I've got them up the wazoo . . ."

"So, you keep them in your ass?

But now you have so many,

they're just coming out on their own . . . ?"

"That's right."

Now obviously,

we don't actually have these items in our asses.

We just want to make sure we mention our ass in every conversation.

And why not?

"It's no skin off my ass . . .

In fact, why don't you shove it up your ass?

As long as I've got them coming out of my ass.

And maybe if you got off your ass . . .

You wouldn't need to be riding my ass."

Some people don't know how to work it in the conversation.

So they just go,

"My ass."

Non-Statements

What about the people you're here with tonight?

You have to get rid of them at some point.

How are you going to do it?

You've got to wrap it up somehow, right?

I hate that extra three and a half minutes at the end

where people just tack on all these statements

that have been formulated to be things no one can disagree with, like,

"Well, you never know . . .

. . . time will tell . . .

. . . we'll see what happens . . .

. . . that's for sure . . ."

Yeah, I think we all know that.

We all know,

the Future is not here yet.

A baby that's five minutes old understands this.

He's born.

He looks around.

He thinks,

"Well, hopefully my neck will firm up.

My balls will drop down.

I'll take it from there.

I'll see what happens . . ."

———

People that have nothing to contribute to the conversation
pipe up about that.

"Not to the best of my knowledge."

"What does that mean?

You don't know?"

"I didn't say that.

I said, I have knowledge.

And it's all not about this."

———

I like when people go,

"What was I saying . . . ? What was I saying . . . ?"

Oh. So, even you're not paying attention to this?

And I'm supposed to be taking notes?

———

My favorite Non-statement is "I want to say."

"What time is that plane coming in . . . ?"

"I want to say . . . nine o'clock . . . ?"

"You want to say?

Well, congratulations, I think you said it.

What's the name of the guy we're supposed to pick up?"

"I want to say . . . Karl."

"So, we have no chance of finding this person?"

"Not to the best of my knowledge."

"Well, you never know.

Time will tell.

We'll see what happens."

Coffee Says

Here's the mathematical equation of coffee.

You're a little depressed.

Not in great shape.

And didn't get a good night's sleep.

Coffee says,

"I have been training my entire life for this exact moment."

When you are in trouble coffee is there.

What else can you turn to?

Lemonade?

Tea?

I hate tea.

Hate it.

It acts like it can do something.

Hot. Same cup.

Can't do a god damned thing.

See through tinted water?

Lemon slices and string?

You have to try and grab that wet, little gross bag as it's swinging around.

Get out of my face.

We need coffee.

You ever hear anybody say,

"I need some tea"?

No.

Nobody needs it.

Need coffee.

Coffee's made from dirt.

Grounds.

You can feel the anger when it's

inside the coffee machine.

Bubbling and hissing in there

like a little volcano.

You look inside, things are spitting out everywhere.

You take one sip, and the coffee's just,

"That's it.

I'm running this outfit now.

I want constant talking.

Endless peeing.

Large intestine, I want all of that out of here right now.

I said, 'Move it.'

Move your bowels.

Shut your mouth.

Drop your pants.

Things are going to be different from now on.

You think I fought my way out of an African jungle,

stowed away on the bottom of a

rusted-out trawler in a burlap

bag to sit in a recycled

paper cup with a

spoon up my ass?

You know what the tattoo on my arm says?

It says, 'Not tea.'"

Coffee Break

The original idea of coffee was a 10-minute break in the middle of eight hours of work.

We're now drinking eight hours of coffee.

Doing 10 minutes of work.

And I think they're more proud of the coffee.

People walk down the street with these cups like they've won an award.

(walking proudly with arm extended out)

"Excuse me, I believe I have the right of way here.

I've got a gigantic coffee . . ."

Alcoholic Coffee Drinks

Alcoholic coffee is a popular type drink.

How rare is that set of circumstances?

Where you need to be whatever the opposite of tired and sober is?

"I am getting trashed and alert TO-NIGHT, I'll tell you that."

"I know my car was all over the road, officer, I saw every second of it.

I know I'll be filling out papers at the Police Station all night.

Bring it on, I'm sharp as a tack.

I am smashed and focused.

I have never felt better or worse in my life."

Or the Red Bulls and vodka.

"I'm going to have a bunch of these and then

just split like an amoeba into two completely different people.

A hyperactive drunk and a slurred speech, bipolar manic depressive.

You can talk to either one you want.

They're both standing right in front of you."

5-Hour Energy Drink

5-Hour Energy Drink.

You ever see that little bottle by the cash register?

5 hours.

5 hours . . . is a weird amount of time.

Who's working 1–6?

What does that even feel like?

To suddenly be in deficit of 5 hours of energy?

"I need 5 hours of energy right now!"

(pant, pant)

If you need 5 hours of energy,

go to bed.

Your day is over.

Pack it in.

Wake up.

Take another run at it tomorrow.

Calm down, dude . . .

You got more than one day.

"I need 5 hours of energy, but I can't drink anything

larger than this.

Do you have a drink in this store,

that big . . . with 5 hours of energy in it?

I can't drink anything larger . . .

I don't have the energy."

———

The workday is 8 hours.

You have an hour for lunch, you're down to 7.

According to this company . . .

I only need 2 hours of natural, human energy and one of their

Meth lab–Hawaiian Punch–Jell-O shots

and I'm good to go.

Cold Beer

I like how the coldness thing drives the beer people crazy.

The commercials are always,

"Frost brewed.

Cold filtered.

Ice bottled.

We pack it in a glacier, then put it on a frozen truck driven by a polar bear."

We're not transplanting a kidney.

You're just trying to get drunk.

Relax, it's going to work.

Orange Juice

Orange juice is never "like fresh squeezed" enough.

I saw on the side of a carton of Tropicana, "now even more like fresh squeezed."

Used to be "like fresh squeezed."

Then, "more like fresh squeezed."

Now, "even more."

Just squeeze it already!

You want it.

We want it.

The oranges are helpless.

Squeeze them up.

Squeeze their little round orange asses and give it to us.

And squeeze the milk out of those almonds too.

Almond Milk

Who got that assignment?

Who had a can of almonds slammed on their desk,

"And find a way to get some milk out of these god damn things.

Nobody wants nuts.

They want milk."

How did they even find a stool small enough to slide under the almonds?

To milk it?

You know how hard it must be to manipulate the teats of an almond?

And rice milk?

Even harder.

Even less room.

Pizza Hut

Everyone's trying to lose a little weight.

Not one person has ever lost one ounce ever.

Do you think one possible explanation might be

that we're still trying to figure out ways to stuff *more* cheese into a piece of pizza?

So far, we've hollowed out the crust and injection-molded that.

That was like three years ago.

Now, they're double layering the foundation

with another layer of cheese beneath the main layer.

So now we have a wall of cheese surrounding the pool of cheese.

The whole god damn thing was cheese to begin with.

Pizza Hut has a new thing coming out . . .

They will actually bake your head right into a block of cheese.

There's no pizza.

It's just cheese coming into every orifice of your skull.

Maybe that'll be enough cheese for us . . .

Raisin Bran

I see the Raisin Bran people are still caught up in their own personal madness.

Still convinced that we're not happy yet with the number of raisins in their product.

Every time I go in the supermarket there is a new announcement on the front of the box,

"More scoops.

Bigger scoops.

Deeper scoops.

Longer scoops.

All raisins, one flake.

COME ON!"

And no one cares.

No one cares about the number of raisins in the god damn
Raisin Bran.

If you're eating Raisin Bran, you've given up on life anyway.

You hate yourself and everyone else.

99% of all Raisin Bran is eaten by people

who have slept over at somebody else's house,

and that's all they had.

No one's intentionally eating this stuff.

"You got any cereal?"

"We got Raisin Bran."

". . . All right . . . (sigh) . . . just give me the Raisin Bran."

Haggar Slacks

I saw an ad for Haggar Slacks.

They're making pants now,

where there's a thing in the front of the pants that you pull,

and the waistband pops open an extra couple of inches,

in the middle of your meal.

That's where we are at now, my friends.

We can't wait until tomorrow to put on bigger pants.

"I need a ripcord right now!

BLAM—

Let me see the dessert menu.

I'm going for it."

Cookies

Different foods affect you at different times of day.

Cookies wait for night.

I've never seen a cookie in the morning. I don't know where they are.

Cookies know in the morning, you are strong, they are weak.

At night you are weak, they are strong.

That's why most cookies are round, because this is a face-to-face confrontation.

You can almost feel their little chocolate chip eyes on you.

Something happens between 9:00 and 11:30 . . .

You're talking to someone,

their face turns into a cookie.

You look away, the clock is a cookie. The moon is a cookie.

Cookie companies make cookies seem very innocent,

"It's just elves living in trees. They make them as a hobby . . ."

They always put happy clowns and balloons on the box.

The truth is cookies should have names like "Chocolate Sons of Bitches."

That's what our real relationship is.

"Those little 'Vanilla Bastards' got me again last night.

And I told you to stop buying those 'Go to Hell Wafers' with the 'Screw You Cream' inside.

I didn't stand a chance."

It's a war.

That's why the cookies live like military.

Inside boxes in those pre-formed Army barracks housing.

You slide it out, it's like a D-day beach-landing troop carrier.

All the cookies are lined up waiting to go into combat.

But I prefer the box over the bag of cookies.

Where they're all just climbing all over each other,

just complete anarchy and chaos.

You get to the end of a row of cookies,

I don't care how crazy you are,

you stop for a second and go,

"What the hell am I doing here?

I was going to have a couple.

I just mowed down a whole row.

And now I'm thinking about going over the wall."

You jump that wall,

you're just a convict running through a cornfield now.

You go back in your kitchen the next morning,

it's like an intersection where there was a car accident.

Broken glass cookie crumbs.

Chocolate skid marks on the napkin.

The milk carton's flat, totaled in the bottom of the trash.

"Boy, I was lucky to walk away from those cookies.

Good thing I had my Haggar Safety Pop-Open slacks."

Gym

I was supposed to go to the gym today.

I did not go.

That's okay.

I know most of you didn't go either.

It is not hard to not go to the gym.

I think we can say,

it is probably the easiest thing in the world to not do.

What do you have to do to not go to the gym?

Nothing.

Just let a little time go by and go,

"Oh well, I can't go now—

I was going to go.

That's what I was doing.

But the time. No time.

It's now not possible for me to go."

———

I have thought,

I should join a gym that's closer.

So I could go more often.

But I wouldn't.

I would just wait longer.

To be able to not go to that one.

———

I like when people say,

"I want to start going to the gym."

So, why don't you go?

"I don't know.

I just don't *want* to go."

But you want to go?

"Oh yes, I definitely want to go."

Have you ever gone?

"No. Not one time. Ever.

But I want to."

So, I think what you're saying is,

what you want,

is to want to go . . . ?

"YES. I want to want to go."

So go . . .

"I don't want to."

The Chair

You have an ass.

What do you think that is?

It's a portable cushioned seating area

that we bring with us at all times.

The ass proves we are slowly

evolving into chairs.

We needed to be comfortable.

And we needed something we could not forget.

"Now, what did I do with my ass?

Oh. I have my ass.

Never mind, I have it.

I found it.

I had my ass with me the whole time."

That is the brilliance of the ass.

Can't get lost.

Even if someone says,

"Get your ass out of here."

You can't do it.

You have to leave with it.

The Strip

But that "needing news" feeling never leaves you that,

"Something's going on. What is going on?"

Even though you check every 11 seconds on the phone.

I want to hear the anchor person talk. I like to hear talking.

Even though I have to read the strip on the bottom at the same time.

Which you cannot do.

If I'm listening to the guy, I miss what it says on the strip.

I'm reading the strip, I miss what the guy says.

"What did he say?

What did that say?

What did that say?

What did she say?"

Which is the news?

The guy or the strip?

Which just happened?

Why can't the guy just tell me what it says on the strip?

Don't these idiots that do the news understand?

We don't want to read.

That's why we're watching TV.

Earpiece

Everybody on the news has that little earpiece.

I notice it's got that expandable, spiral phone cord that goes down their neck.

But why would it need to expand?

How far is this guy's head going from the top of his shirt

that he needs that much expanding wire?

Is he a newsman or a kitchen phone?

The Crisis

They always feel they should go to somebody

that's closer physically to whatever it is.

"Maybe they know something . . ."

So, they go to that person,

"Well, Jim, there's nothing happening here yet.

There's no one here.

I have no information.

And I can't see a god damn thing.

I don't even know if this is where I'm supposed to be.

Back to you in the studio."

They go back to the studio

where they've already come up with a logo for the crisis.

"We need a font."

The logo always looks a little bit like the crisis.

If there's a guy that's under fire,

you see the guy and you see the fire.

The worst crisis is when the letters in the word "Crisis"

start to crack and break apart.

There's pieces missing from the "C" and the "R" and the "I."

That's a bad crisis.

The word "crisis" is in crisis from the crisis.

And that's when it's time to take an instant poll on the Internet.

"Let's get the perspective of a group of people even dumber than we are.

The general public."

No News

I live in the fantasy, watching News,

that there still is News.

But what don't we know?

Nothing.

There's nothing we don't know.

Everybody's on everything every second.

They even start the News saying,

"Well, I'm sure you've all seen this by now . . . "

The word "News" means new.

So, if it's not new there's No News.

They used to say,

No News is Good News.

But now,

All News is No News.

Which is,

Bad News for News,

I think.

Which you maybe already knew.

But to me, that's Big News.

If what we all thought of as News

is now No News,

Huge News.

I mean come on,

the End of News is the

biggest thing that ever happened.

That's your lead story.

Old News

The Worst News is definitely anything thought of as Old News.

History is fine. But if it's in the past and not yet history, don't ever talk about that.

People go, "Oh my god, that was like a week ago, what's wrong with you?"

Break-in

I need Breaking.

We want Breaking.

Break-in

They always say, "I'm sorry to break in—"

Which they're not, they love it. They feel important

and they get to screw up the person

they work with and secretly hate.

"But we have a breaking story,

it just broke.

We're going to go to a break.

Then after the break we're going to

break it down and we're going to

go straight through without a break.

Unless something else breaks,

then we'll have to break away,

break that, which will be

followed by another break

because we're about

to go broke."

Weather Girls

And what's with all the heated up, sexed out, Super Vixen weather girls

wearing insane cocktail outfits on local TV at 9:30 in the morning?

Everyone else on the news looks normal.

They go to weather, it's like a private Vegas sex club.

Masks and whips and thigh-high boots.

She's spanking the traffic guy with a riding crop.

The Doppler's brought to you by Crotchless Underwear.

Turn down the heat.

You got 100 million men in this country

trying to be extremely respectful

while adjusting to new guidelines

just handed down in a very fluid situation.

You can help out a little.

Shoulder your weapons before noon.

Is that fair?

Sports Watch

I love to watch sports.

One of the things I enjoy most about sports is not the game,

but hearing all the things I already know about the game

repeated back to me over and over again

after the game.

I've got to watch the postgame show.

The highlights.

The analysis.

The call-in show.

Do I not really believe that I saw the game?

You should see me tearing the paper apart every morning

to get to the sports section,

just so I can go,

"Aha! I knew what I saw is what happened when I was watching it."

What is this urge to keep finding out information I already have?

It's like when I drive by a mirrored office building.

I always look at the reflection to see if I'm in the car.

And what would I do if I looked, and there was a small Korean woman driving my car?

If I look at my watch and then one second later, someone asks me what time it is?

I look again.

When you came in here tonight,

How many times did you look at your ticket?

Five?

Eight?

Human brain's a sieve.

Why do you think they run the same commercial 150 times?

I'm trying to save money on car insurance.

I want to wear an untucked shirt.

I don't know how to do it.

Gambling in Vegas

I gamble a little.

I'd probably gamble more, but I don't win so I stop.

I don't understand gambling addiction.

I don't find losing money addictive.

My brain works like,

LOSING MONEY: STOP ACTIVITY

MAKING MONEY: CONTINUE ACTIVITY

Besides which, you really think you're supposed to win these games?

Losing money is what gambling is.

When you leave a building with more money, that's your job.

Think about what this place would be like if it was easy to win the games.

It would be very different.

You think the traffic's bad on the strip now?

That beautiful casino out there would be a cinder block bunker with a communal toilet.

You think they'd have nice restaurants?

You'd be lucky to get those orange crackers with the peanut butter in between.

And when you called down to the front desk

instead of them saying, "Have a lucky day,"

they'd go, "Why don't you just shove it up your ass?"

That's what it would be like if you could win the games.

Cremation

I hear a lot of people say they want to be cremated.

Definitely a shift in how people are looking at their lives.

People used to want a big block of granite.

Their name carved into it with a chisel.

"I was here, god damn it!"

Cremation's like you're trying to cover up a crime.

"Burn the body, scatter the ashes.

As far as anyone's concerned,

this whole thing never happened."

I would not want to be cremated.

It seems impolite.

I feel the least I can do at my own funeral is show up.

Everybody I know is going to be there.

I want to be there too.

Dead as a door nail.

Laid out like a six-foot party sub.

At a regular funeral, there's still a chance the person could wake up . . .

Not at a cremation.

A cremation is like,

"That ashtray's full.

This party's over."

Glad Sandwich Bags

I still can't believe that every single day of my life

I see people picking up their dog's defecation with their hands.

Every day of my life.

The confidence they have in that Glad sandwich bag.

Where does that come from?

What do we know about the Glad sandwich bag?

It locks in freshness?

Which, I would think, is the last thing you want to do with a big steaming pile anyway.

I don't know how human beings make these mental leaps.

"Glad keeps a sandwich fresh, I'll pick up feces with it."

I hate just as much, before the event

when I see them walking their dog,

and my eye goes right to that suspicious little tuft of plastic or paper clutched in their other hand.

and I know exactly what's going to happen . . .

If aliens are watching this through telescopes,

they're going to think the dogs are the leaders of the planet.

If you see two life forms,

one of them takes a crap,

and the other one's carrying it for him . . .

Who would you assume is in charge of that society?

Nose Hair

I'd like to say something to all the men in the audience about nose hair.

. . . And that should be all I need to say.

There should be no further comment necessary.

The term nose hair should be a medical term, completely unknown to the general public.

I had a meeting with a lawyer the other day,

and I'm telling you this guy really had a situation.

If a spark came off a match, we could have had a brush fire in there.

This guy's a lawyer.

Somewhat of a public image profession.

And he's giving me his opinions.

There's no opinions when you've got scarecrow straw coming out.

There's only one opinion: Objection.

"You, sir, are beyond the nostril perimeter."

I want to know how this slipped by final inspection,

before walking out of the house.

If you glanced in the hubcap of a passing car

one could easily see,

. . . there's a problem.

Itching, Burning and Redness

Doctors on TV always have these

"Itching, burning and redness" pads on their desk.

With a little check-off box next to each word . . .

What kind of a doctor gets pads like this professionally printed up?

Goes into a stationery store,

"I need itching, burning and redness pads.

This is happening a lot in my office

and I want to check them off as they happen."

"Nurse, send in the next patient please,

do you have itching?"

"Yes."

"Burning?"

"Yes."

"Redness?"

"Yes."

"Hold it right there.

That's all the boxes I have.

Thank you for helping me use my little pad.

(tears off paper and hands to patient)

Good luck with your disgusting situation."

Suicide Bomber

My favorite suicide bomber's the guy

who accidentally blows himself up without injuring anyone else in the area.

A Jihad E. Coyote kind of guy.

I guess I just wish we could see that moment of,

"Is it the red button, then the green? Oh no, wait . . ."

Eventually they'll have roller skates.

Huge rocket on the back, trying to light it.

"It better work this time.

The last one I did a loop-de-loop right into a wall.

Then I slid slowly down it totally embarrassed."

Terrorist Monkey Bars

One of the things we do have on our side in this war is

we seem to have a lot of films of terrorist groups in their training camps.

I don't know how we got these films but we got them.

And I think one of the main things we can learn from watching these films,

is the tremendous emphasis the terrorists place on the monkey bars.

Has there ever been a war where the decisive battle was fought on a children's playground?

"I need a volunteer to gain control of that horse with the giant spring underneath it."

I think we ought to focus more on the seesaw.

We've got so many fat kids in this country,

that could sit on one end and keep those skinny terrorists up in the air on the other.

You threaten to jump off of the bottom of a seesaw.

That's some terrorism.

"Hey, let me down, let me down."

"Let's see your shoe bombs work now."

Slightly Nazi

There's a particular motorcycle helmet I see a lot on the streets lately that I don't get.

And I'm sure you know the one I'm going to say.

It has that unmistakable flare around the back.

I wouldn't say that it's full Nazi,

but it is definitely slightly Nazi.

And these are not hardcore bikers I'm talking about.

I'm talking scooters, with the little knees-together riding position.

How do seemingly normal people get themselves into a Nazi shopping situation?

You walk in the motorcycle store, the man says,

"May I help you?"

You go,

"Yes, I need a motorcycle helmet."

He says,

"Well, I have these regular ones here."

You go,

"Ahh, what else is there . . . ?"

He says,

"Well, let me ask you this . . .

How do you feel about the Nazis?"

You go,

"To tell the truth, I wasn't crazy about the genocide, hatred, racism and mass murder."

He says, "What about the helmets?"

"The helmets weren't bad.

I can't really say I had a problem with the helmet as a stand-alone item."

And interestingly, there is another type of helmet I've seen

that is kind of a small black plastic circle,

which actually looks like the yarmulke that religious Jewish people wear.

I think I see a theme emerging here . . .

I guess if you're a motorcycle rider,

and you're a WWII fan,

and you're in the market for a motorcycle helmet,

we got you covered either way you want to go.

Car Horn

People love the car horn because they know they could never think of enough curse words

to last as long as they can just hold that button down.

"Wait'll they hear THIS . . ."

We also believe for some reason that the harder we actually push our finger on the button,

the more effect the horn is going to have.

I love when we try and affect inanimate objects that way.

Like when the car doesn't start,

people always try turning the key really hard.

Like the key is going to go,

"Oww, alright. I get it."

Directions Voice

When people give you directions in the car they use different voices too.

They have a story voice and a directions voice.

"I don't think I even want to go out with her again.

Make a right at the next corner.

I think she might be a wacko.

Watch this guy pulling out. He doesn't see you.

I'm really just sick of dating at this point.

The bridge is out. We just went off a cliff.

I don't know. Maybe I'll call her.

The car's a huge ball of flames. Our lives are over."

OnStar

Or the

"OnStar service,

available now on GM vehicles."

OnStar satellites orbiting the Earth.

OnStar technicians wearing headsets

at the Command Control Center

beaming signals back and forth across the galaxy,

all because you can't keep from locking yourself out of your own damn car?

Is this really why we conquered space?

To help out all these puddin' heads in mall parking lots,

looking in their car window going,

". . . Oh, there they are.

(calling across parking lot)

They're in the car . . .

That's why it's still running.

No, forget the two-cent wire hanger.

I'll contact a zillion-dollar Deep Space Communication Center instead.

They bounce a signal off of Neptune.

It's a lot easier that way."

OnStar . . .

They should call this service, Moron Star.

That's what it really is.

You hit the button.

They answer,

"Yes, moron. What did you do now?"

"Well, I got lost.

Then I crashed.

I'm hanging off the side of a cliff by the seatbelt

. . . and I'm trying to find a good Italian restaurant."

"All right, moron. Take it easy, we'll walk you through it . . ."

Opposite Clothes

For some reason humans like to dress in clothes

that are the exact opposite of who they really are.

Can't play the sport?

Wear the jersey.

Morbidly obese?

Walk around in a jogging outfit.

No talent, skills or ability of any kind?

Put on a fancy suit.

Announce you're running for office,

and would like to be in charge of everything.

Liberace

I saw this thing on Liberace on TV.

Apparently, Liberace made his limo driver, who was also his lover,

get all this plastic surgery so he would look like a young Liberace.

And he was on the show and he looked just like a young Liberace.

I definitely see two potential problems here with this.

First, creating a living, breathing, human blow-up doll in your own likeness

so you can sodomize yourself as a young man.

That's number one.

Number two,

getting involved with someone you work with.

That can get awkward too.

They must have had some weird fights.

"Listen, buddy.

You being the new me may be new to you,

but it's getting pretty old to me.

And don't look at me like me when I'm talking to you."

Movie Garbage

Took the kids to the movies the other day.

New announcement in the movie theater

I had not seen before,

"Please pick up the garbage from around your seat after the movie."

"Oh, okay.

Maybe I'll bring my orange jumpsuit and wooden stick with a nail in it too.

Maybe I'll work my way down the highway after the credits roll."

I'm not picking nothing up.

I'm the one that threw it down.

Because we have a deal in place with the movie theater people.

The deal is,

you're ripping us off.

In exchange for that, when I'm done with something,

I open my hand.

And let it roll down eight rows.

I am not sticking my hand down into that dark, scary hole

to try and pry out three Goobers that have been soda-welded there since *The Shawshank Redemption*.

What have they given us?

A cup holder growing out of the armrest?

Is that our "luxury feature"?

How about an automatic popcorn shooter?

That fires one in every five seconds?

To complete this corpse-like experience.

Grip

The cup holder.

That is the object that defines our culture.

We're not holding cups.

Too much strain on the hand.

Give me a belt clip for the cell phone.

Give me an earpiece so I don't have to hold the phone up.

And not one that I have to take in and out.

Just drill it right into the side of my skull.

———

If I have two beers at a ballgame,

give me a hat where I can put one in each side

with a feeding tube coming down.

If you've got a dog, you've got a leash with

extra leash wound up inside,

in case he pulls it,

I just let the line out like he's a marlin.

I go on Amazon, I set one-click ordering.

One click.

That's it.

You want me to click twice?

I don't even want it anymore.

Public Restroom

I go in a public restroom

I expect a motion detector on the

toilet, sink, urinal

I'm doing nothing in here.

Why is the sink never as aware of us as the toilet?

You always have to go into a David Copperfield magic act to get that to work.

Go over to the paper towels,

do another "Dance of the Seven Veils" over there.

And why, by the way,

are public restrooms constructed from the most sound-reflective materials on earth?

Metal, glass, rock-hard tile?

So that every tiny human noise is rendered in Dolby ProLogic Surround Sound quality?

Is it not bad enough in there?

Who designed the bathroom stall?

With the under-display viewing windows?

So, we can all see the pathetic, collapsed pant legs

And tragic little shoe fronts just barely poking out from underneath?

The impotent belt just lying there . . .

How much more money is it to bring this wall down another foot?

It's the cheapest wall in the world.

It's a metal panel.

They don't even make the panels meet up *tight* in the corners.

Why can't they cinch that up?

"You got a gap in a bad spot, dude."

Sometimes you're walking by, you see a frightened terrorized human eye.

Just a flash of eye-white in space.

A darting pupil.

I'm not a horse.

I don't want to be in a stall.

If it's a stall, why don't I hang my head over the front door?

That's what the horses do.

I'm sure my co-workers recognize my shoes,

let's let them see my face too.

"Hey, Bob, how you doing?

Yeah, this is why I had to run out of that big meeting . . .

Had a little PowerPoint presentation of my own to do . . ."

All Awards Are Stupid

"HBO COMEDIAN AWARD" ACCEPTANCE SPEECH:

At moments like this, I like to quote my good friend Carl Reiner, who has often said to me,

"You don't give awards to comedians."

First of all, comedians don't need awards.

Awards are for people that are looking for work.

We're not looking for work.

If you're any good as a comedian you've got tons of work.

We've all got wrinkled suits and smelly shirts from packing and unpacking

and schlepping all over the god damned country doing 10 million different kinds of gigs.

More importantly, your whole career as a comedian is about making fun

of pretentious, high-minded, self-congratulatory, BS events like this one.

The whole feeling in this room of reverence and honoring

is the exact opposite of everything I have wanted my life to be about.

I really don't even want to be up here.

I want to be in the back somewhere saying something funny

to someone about what a crock this whole thing is.

And I don't want to give the wrong impression

that I'm not very honored by this, because I am.

But it doesn't change the truth, which is this:

All awards are stupid.

Every real estate office has some Five Star President's Award plaque.

Every hotel check-in has some Gold Circle Service thing.

Every car salesman is a Platinum Jubilee Winner.

And it's all a big jerk-off.

The hotel stinks.

The real estate person is stupid.

And the only thing the car salesman is good at is ripping you off.

Because the awards don't mean a god damn thing.

They're all stupid.

How many more times are we going to feel the need to set aside a night

to give out these jag-off bowling trophies so all these people can congratulate each other on

how much money they're making, boring the piss out of half the world?

And if I hadn't already won all these awards I would not be talking like this . . .

The truth is that the comedians should be the only ones getting awards.

We're the only ones that have to actually think of something original and funny and interesting for ourselves to say.

I don't know why we are so fascinated by actors in this culture.

They haven't got a thought in their stupid bedhead hairdo.

"We must honor this man.

Why, he pretended to be Bill Jones.

He's a genius, I tell you."

Roll the cameras.

Put on these clothes.

Stand on this spot.

Ready . . . ?

And say what we told you to say.

He did it!

Give him a huge golden trophy.

He's a god damn genius.

Walking down the red carpet in these ridiculous outfits like they're Senators from Krypton.

I should bring some of these things so you can see how stupid they really are.

The Golden Globe.

It looks like something you'd get for third place in a pie-eating contest.

It's about this big . . .

The plaque on the front is the thinnest fake, yellow metal in the world.

It's glued on crooked.

The glue is coming out around the sides.

My name isn't even spelled right, it's Seinfield.

No one cares.

It doesn't matter.

The Audience Decides

(AN AUDIENCE AD LIB AT THE COMEDY CELLAR ONE NIGHT)

You all get to make the decision if something is funny or not.

All these people come up here with all their experience and their TV credits and their careers.

And you decide.

And what the hell do you know about it?

Nothing.

You're not funny.

You've never written a joke.

If you were funny, you wouldn't need to come to this.

You're not even really paying attention.

But it's your call.

That's the system.

And as comedians we accept it.

But think how you'd feel if I just came into your office and went,

"I don't agree with the things you say in these meetings.

I don't know anything about your business.

I don't even work here.

I just thought I'd come in off the street and give you a piece of my mind.

What gives me the authority?

I bought two drinks."

Your Job

I don't know the occupation of one person in this audience.

I don't know where you work.

I've never set foot in your place of business, but I know one thing about your job.

I know, wherever you work, you cannot believe how dumb the system they have there is.

"How did they get so many idiots in one place?

And this new nincompoop that's in charge of these morons

is an even bigger pinhead than the last jerk those numbnuts hired.

I'd quit but I could never make the same money someplace else

doing as little work as I do here.

Are you kidding?

I love it here, I do nothing.

I just don't understand why the company's doing so bad."

The Offensive Brain

Why does the brain do that?

Why as we try our best throughout the day to act normal and pretend to be not weird,

why is your brain always thinking of obnoxious comments that you *could* make?

Rude behaviors, inappropriate actions that would only horrify, disturb and offend.

Why?

Where do these thoughts come from?

"Why not trip this person carrying a large box that can't quite see where they're going?"

Why does my brain present me with these options?

"What if I stood up in this important meeting

and made an outrageous sexual overture that would get me instantly fired?"

Are you ever in the middle of a conversation with someone and think,

"I could probably kill this guy right now.

He'd never see it coming.

He asked me to hand him a scissor.

What if I took that scissor and stabbed him with it?"

Why do I have suicide fantasies to go along with my homicide fantasies?

I go over to someone's place that has a terrace or a balcony.

I always have to go out on it, look over the edge, and think,

"Oh, I could fall right over this thing.

Everybody here would freak out."

"Oh my god, he killed himself?

I can't believe it.

. . . I was just about to stab him with a scissor."

Everything Is Garbage

I believe that all of the objects and possessions that we own

really just exist at different stages of becoming garbage.

To me, the world is comprised of garbage and pre-garbage.

I hate the garbage, and I love to throw it out.

That is my personality type.

I love to throw anything out.

I find if I have something, I really don't want it.

I wish there was a store where you could buy something,

pivot, and just throw it down a chute into an incinerator.

Complete the whole inevitable process right there.

I like to walk the streets of New York.

If a garbage man says to me, "Love your work,"

I go, "Right back at you."

Because every object on earth is actually part of a giant, slow parade to the dumpster.

While you're walking into your house excitedly with your shopping bags,

the garbage man is driving by in his truck.

And he looks at you like, "Oh, I'll see you soon."

Your home is really just a Garbage Processing Center.

You buy new things

You bring them into your house

and you slowly Trashify them over time . . .

A new purchase in the house begins its life full of hope and promise.

The box is opened on the kitchen table.

The Place of Honor for the New Arrival.

You read the instructions.

You fill out the registration card.

You may even join the club of other idiots that have this thing.

You repeat some of the lines the salesman used on you.

But they don't sound the same when you say them.

And you start to realize that maybe you're not going to be quite as keen on drying out fruit and

storing it in your basement

as you thought you were going to be.

From there it is demoted to the closet.

That's why we have that.

So we don't have to see all of the huge mistakes we have made.

It starts on a shelf, where it's easy to get to.

Then to the floor, where you start to step on it to reach things.

It's cracking and breaking under your foot.

You don't even give a damn.

Because you're now only interested in some other, newer item that is just beginning on its Journey to Junk.

The next step down for the object is the garage,

one of the longest phases in Trashification.

But one of the most definite.

No object in human history has ever successfully made it

OUT of the garage and BACK into the house.

Even the word "garage" seems to be a form of the word "gar-bage."

Once you're living in the same room as the garbage cans,

well . . . it won't be much longer now.

Really eBay is the only thing that can save the object at this point.

eBay, of course, another great step forward in human culture.

"Hey, why don't we mail our garbage back and forth to each other?"

"No, no, Jerry, you don't understand.

The things I get on eBay, they're collectibles."

"Oh, I see.

So you purchased this item from a collector

who collects these collectibles because even he didn't want it."

Or the personal storage area.

This is the saddest of all.

Now instead of free garbage, you pay rent to visit your garbage.

It's like a prison visit.

Everything is rusted and broken.

You lift up that rolling steel door, make your little speech.

"Listen, I am trying to get you guys out of here.

There's no place for you in the world right now.

That's why you are incarcerated.

But I'm working on it, and I will be back."

Everything is thrown out in the end.

Even we are thrown out in the end, my friends.

And when I hear about someone that died and wanted some important personal possessions put in with them when they're buried, I am all for that.

Take your crap with you.

They say you can't take it with you.

I say,

"Let's try."

DNA

Why do we try so hard?

Why all the desperado, go for broke, personal attractiveness choices?

Why do we take these chances?

Where is the brain when these decisions are made?

The brain is not involved.

The brain is intelligence. We're not using that.

It's our DNA. That's what's in control.

67 years old.

"Put paint on your head. People will think you're 28."

And color in your eyebrows with a squeaky Sharpie.

DNA says, "Toupee—good thinking."

DNA says, "We're going to get you a cheap wig and a tight girdle and we're going out."

What DNA wants and will do anything for, is to just get itself to the next generation.

DNA stands for Damn Near Attractive and that's all we're trying to get you up to.

Conceived

My wife and I conceived sometime in January.

I love the term "conceived."

It makes it sound like I actually thought of something.

"Yes, I conceived of the whole thing."

"Is that your child?"

"No, it's just an idea I had."

Baby Born

So, the way they do it is they have this huge sheet.

And I am positioned north of the equator.

The baby's born.

The doctor picks the baby up.

Her head just pops up from behind this sheet.

It's like a *Kukla, Fran and Ollie* show.

So, instead of experiencing the most poignant moment of my life,

I'm thinking,

"This is the greatest puppet show I've ever seen.

It's so lifelike.

And it's got my face in it."

Baby Products

Why does every single baby product in the world have to have a picture of a baby on it?

The food, the toys, the wipes.

We know it's for babies.

Is anyone buying Huggies by mistake?

"Hey, these aren't elegant dinner napkins.

This is, like, for a baby's ass or something."

Birthday Clown

I go to these kids' parties . . .

The birthday party clown always corners me

and wants to talk to me about his comedy career.

I don't know what to tell him.

"Listen, dude,

I don't know how to get from these parties to having your own show on TV.

I just went from having my own show on TV to these parties myself.

I don't know how to do it in reverse."

———

I think the hardest part of being a clown,

would be that you are constantly referred to as a clown.

"Who is that clown?"

"I'm not working with that clown."

"Did you hire that clown?"

"The guy's a clown."

How do you even know that you want to be a clown?

I guess you just get to a point where your pants look so bad

it's actually easier to become a clown than have the proper alterations done.

Birthday Kids Jumpy Castle

Then they have this other thing at these parties

called a Jumpy Castle.

Basically,

it's a small portable insane asylum for children.

You insert your child into the slot.

The child turns around and shows you what their real personality actually is.

By the time they get out,

they're in such a psychotic frenzy,

all you can do is just load them back into your minivan-paddy-wagon,

strap them into their little car seat straitjacket and drive away.

"Go ahead and scream, you're out of your mind anyway."

Circus

This is why the circus is still around after 15 centuries of no one enjoying five seconds of it.

Parents think kids like it.

Kids think, "I guess my parents needed me to see this for some reason."

No one's got the guts to stand up in the middle of a circus and go,

"What the hell is this even supposed to be?"

Watching flexible immigrants fleeing for their lives

from these deranged animals

jacked up on Thorazine trying to survive

on a diet of sawdust and peanut shells.

No one's laughing at the clowns.

Because we all know somewhere underneath all that bright color,

there is a man who is not right.

And I don't want to be too down on the clowns.

We are colleagues in a certain sense.

I think a certain professional respect is appropriate.

Annoying Line

And I would love to tell you some stories about all the cute little things

that our new daughter does.

But I'm not going to do that.

Because I'm not exactly sure where the "annoying line" is.

I know it's right around me somewhere here.

And I also know it's very easy to cross,

because I sure as hell don't want to hear about all the funny things your kid said.

Or did.

And how you "don't know where he gets it from."

I'll tell you where he gets it from.

He gets it from you.

Because you're boring.

He's boring.

Your whole damn family is boring.

———

I would like to hear the parents of dumb kids

talk about how they always know exactly where the kid is getting it from.

"We've tried everything.

MTV, rap music, the Internet.

He's just not picking up anything that surprises us in any way.

He never says anything that we don't know exactly where he got it from."

Family Member Stickers

I would describe myself as very "pro" family.

Very "anti" wanting to hear anything about anybody else's family.

Particularly regarding the row of little white family member stick figures,

on the back window of your minivan.

No one's going,

"Hey, look, three girls and a ferret.

Let's catch up and find out more."

"There's two lesbians, a Rottweiler and a Korean kid.

I want to meet them.

Let's congratulate them on those very specific choices."

———

We don't need to know more.

We see you're in a minivan.

Doesn't that tell us enough?

You're just trying to get a group of people from birth to death

as comfortably and efficiently as possible.

———

I'm also not seeing any stick figures getting out of these vehicles either, by the way.

I'm seeing the bumper come up about a foot and a half when they disembark.

How about some stickers on the backs of some of these fat asses?

"Cake, fries, soda, pudding pops, Ho Hos, Clark bar."

They seem to be part of the family too.

Daddy's Home

There are two basic male domestic instincts.

First, we see our daily return to the home as an event of great momentousness.

We announce it at the door, "Daddy's home!"

As if family members will drop to their knees

and weep at their good fortune.

They do not.

Because they know once our coat is off,

that concludes our involvement with anyone or anything in the house.

Which is the second male domestic instinct:

Avoidance.

The only thing ever heard about Dad around the house is,

"Where . . . is . . . your . . . father?

I saw him at the wedding,

and that is the last we know of his whereabouts . . ."

In the '50s fathers spent a lot of time working on bomb shelters.

They'd be underground digging huge holes in their own backyards

more comfortable dealing with a nuclear holocaust than a nuclear family.

Golf

Avoidance is the male domestic instinct.

Golf the ultimate avoidance activity.

A game so nonsensically difficult

so pointless

so irrationally time-consuming.

The word "GOLF" could only possibly stand for,

"Get Out Leave Family."

And I have a lot of friends that play.

They all love to play.

"You would love it, Jerry . . .

It's—a—very—challenging—game . . ."

Yes. I am sure that it is.

It's also challenging trying to throw a Tic Tac

100 yards into a shoebox.

In the fantasy mind of the golfing father,

when he comes home,

the family will come running out,

to hear the exciting stories,

of his golfing adventures.

In reality:

No one is even aware that he has left or returned.

From 8½ hours of idiotic hacking

through sand and weeds,

while driving drunk in a clown car

through a fake park.

Kids in Bed

My wife has been bringing our youngest one in the bed

every night at 3 o'clock in the morning.

This is another beautiful experience.

It's like sleeping next to a laundry bag that has

a live goat tied up inside.

All night long the goat is punching and kicking, trying to get out.

He has somehow mounted himself onto a rotating display wheel that works its way around the bed

raising his body temperature to 189 degrees.

How does that little body pump out all that heat?

God, it's hot in there . . .

And not only is it romantic to sleep with your wife like that,

but you wake up feeling refreshed and ready to go.

The Idea of Dad

It takes time for the idea of dad to sink in.

It was years into my children's lives I'd see them looking at me

from across the room like they were going to

come over and say,

"I'm sorry, is someone helping you . . . ?

Mom, the horsey ride guy's here again.

Do we need anything?"

Thank You Monkey

Why do all parents now have to turn their kids

into battery powered, cymbal clapping, thank you monkeys?

"Thank the yogurt lady.

Thank the bus driver.

Thank the man for not abducting you and making you grow up in a tent in his backyard.

(clapping cymbals)

Thank you. Thank you. Thank you. Thank you."

They do this because all they want

is for some other parent to say,

"Oh, your child has such good manners."

No, he doesn't.

He doesn't know what's going on.

When trained poodles walk around on their hind legs, they don't think,

"Oh, look at me! I'm progressing to a higher level of species."

They think,

"I don't want any more beatings, so I'm going to do this."

Mob Boss

When I say I love being a parent,

I certainly don't mean to give you the impression that I am in any way effective at it.

I tell my kids to do things.

But they say, "No."

And so I have been reduced to threats, fear and intimidation.

I have become a small-time mob boss around my house.

I figure out what they like, and then I threaten to hurt those things.

"I notice you're becoming quite fond of that little stuffed Curious George

that sits in the corner of your room.

It would certainly be a shame if something were to suddenly happen to him.

He sits so close to the stairwell.

And with you being at nursery school all day.

He seems so vulnerable.

I was just looking at the box he came in,

and I think I noticed the word 'flammable.' "

Sometimes they make little Play-Doh animals.

And when they go to sleep at night,

I break the heads off of the animals,

and leave them at the foot of their bed for them to discover

when they wake up in the morning.

Nothing wrong with sending your child a little Sicilian message once in a while.

Other Kids over My House

Sometimes they bring kids over my house,

which I don't get.

"We have kids.

Why do we need these other kids?"

Do you find that other people's children . . . never look quite right?

Their faces always seem Silly Puttied into some compressed or elongated shape.

Too wide. Too narrow.

"Is that boy's head supposed to be like that?

He's a melon head . . ."

Then the parents come to pick him up . . .

"Oh, they're melon heads, too.

It's just a big melon head family.

He's fine."

Most children I meet are either sticky or crusty.

I think they start off sticky,

roll in whatever debris,

it adheres to them,

and they become crusty.

To me, all these kids that are coming over my house are just Pecan Logs that talk.

I have never felt concerned when these little kids would hurt themselves

while they are in my home.

"Well, sure you're crying, you just drove your head into the side of that television set.

. . . That was the damnedest thing I've ever seen, by the way.

No hesitation. You lowered your melon head and went right into it.

That's a very valuable lesson you just received.

You learned, Dumb = Pain.

You're going to be learning this many, many times in your life, I have a feeling.

Because when you're dumb, life hurts."

Star Wars

I watch a lot of *Star Wars* with the kids.

Don't care for it, personally.

I can say that publicly because they were never going to put me in *Star Wars* anyway.

I'm wrong for the tone.

You don't want a character that during one of the lightsaber fights says,

"You know, all these backflips, splits and cartwheels?

No one is scared of anyone that can do these things.

You can flip all you want.

It doesn't hurt the other person.

If you want to go to a different platform, just step down to it.

Someone's trying to kill you. You need to focus."

———

I'd like to be in a casual scene with Darth Vader.

I really want to ask him,

"So, are you able to go anywhere without the music?

If you get up in the middle of the night to pee,

does it come blasting on, waking everybody up?

If you stop does the music stop?"

Sucks and Great

Things we do to convince ourselves

that our lives don't suck.

Tomorrow you'll be walking around,

"My life doesn't suck.

I saw a comedian that had a TV show in the '90s last night . . ."

Even though the truth is your life does pretty much suck.

I know that because I know that everyone's life sucks.

Your life sucks, my life sucks too.

Perhaps not quite as much . . .

But in the vast suckness of human living,

everyone's life sucks and that's okay.

Never feel bad that your life sucks.

Because the greatest lesson you can learn in life,

is that "sucks" and "great" are pretty close.

People want you to think that these are the

polar opposite ends of the spectrum, but they're not.

They're right there.

So sick of hearing about some "great" restaurant that everyone says "you have to" go to.

You know how your friends just single you out for some reason?

"*You have to go.*

You would love it.

Wouldn't he love it?

He would love it.

You would love it, yoouu . . .

You have to go because . . . *You.*"

"Did you like it?"

"I didn't care for it myself, but *you.*"

―――

I don't like great.

I'm looking for "Not bad."

"How's the food over there?"

"Not bad . . ."

"That sounds great.

Let's just go there and get this over with."

If you go to a great restaurant,

they've got to tell you the Specials.

"Would you like to hear the Specials . . . ?"

"No.

If they're so Special, put them on the menu.

I'm not interested in food that's auditioning to get on the team."

I don't understand all the words they use, anyway.

"We're going to pan-sear it,

we're going to herb-crust it.

And then we're going to drizzle it with something that's a reduction of something else."

They're always drizzling in these places.

Stop drizzling.

We can't take the drizzling anymore.

"Maybe if you didn't reduce it so much, you wouldn't have to drizzle it."

The meal takes two and a half hours.

Your ass is hurting by the end of it.

It's not half as good as a bowl of Lucky Charms and Pepsi, anyway . . .

The check always comes in that special book like it's

"The Story of the Bill."

Yeah, here's the story:

"Once upon a time, you got ripped."

That's the story.

You're standing on the street afterwards with your friends,

"Was that great . . . ?

I don't know if it was *great* . . .

Actually, I think it sucked.

That great place sucked."

Then you go to a baseball game.

You have a hot dog.

The hot dog is cold.

The bun is not toasted.

The vendor is an ex-con in a work-release program.

You do not care.

You love that hot dog every time.

Does it suck?

Yes.

Is it great?

Yes.

That's how close they are.

Sucks and Great are the only two ratings people even use anymore.

No one's interested in any other opinion.

"Hey, want to go see that new movie? I heard it's great."

"Really? I heard it sucks."

"How could it suck? It was supposed to be great."

"I heard the beginning is great, but after that it sucks."

"Aw, that sucks."

"I know, it could have been great."

I say to you,

that "sucks" and "great" are the exact same thing.

You have an ice-cream cone. You're walking down the street.

The ice cream falls off the top of the cone.

Hits the pavement.

Sucks.

What do you say?

"Great."

The
Teens

Over the course of all these years when I look at all this stuff

it reminds me of my horse-racing bit.

Where the out-of-breath horse doesn't understand why the jockey took them

all around the track, the longest possible route.

He gets to the finish line and says,

"Why didn't we just stay here? We would have been first."

So, the horse has quite a good grasp of the logistics of the racetrack.

But incredibly, so little understanding of the horse race itself.

So smart and so dumb.

And I guess that's me.

It took a lot of effort for me to get all the way around the track to finally discover

the end point is exactly where I wanted to be at the beginning.

So many other avenues have come my way over the years.

And I have taken a visit here and there to the other forms

in which I could press myself into service.

As I write this, we are in the time of corona, so there is no live performing.

Stand-up is about a brief, fleeting moment of human connection.

Like surfers sitting in the water on their board, just waiting

for one more ride.

One more thrilling skim across the top of the world.

People often ask me where I like to work.

What kind of places, theaters, which cities?

The place I like to work is in my head.

To try and reach someone else's.

The special, special thing about stand-up is the sound that tells you for sure that you did it.

You reached them.

Of course, we can never know exactly how all of it really even happens.

We don't need to know everything.

We can feel what's real.

And I hope we get to be together again someday soon.

In the meantime, putting all this together in a book has given us another kind of real connection.

You can feel that it's how we're supposed to be.

Annoying Friends

Why are your friends so annoying?

These are the people you have chosen to be with.

And yet, you cannot stand them.

"Who's going?

How do we get there?

When do we leave?

Where is it again?

Which car? My car? Your car?

One car? Two cars?

Your car's too small.

We can squeeze.

Pick me up? Pick you up?

It's on the way.

It's the opposite direction.

What time is the show?

7 o'clock.

Who the hell has a show at 7 o'clock?

This guy is ruining my entire life.

Are we eating?

Did you eat?

I didn't eat.

I'm starving.

I'm stuffed.

I've been eating Jolly Ranchers all day. I need something solid."

———

Half of you didn't even remember the damn thing was tonight.

You had to be reminded of that . . .

"You know, we're going to that show tonight."

". . . Tonight?"

"Yes, it's tonight."

". . . I don't really feel like going tonight."

"Well, we have to go tonight.

That's the only night he's here.

This guy's huge.

He's here and he's gone.

You think he's going to play here for a month?

We're living in Bakersfield. Snap out of it."

Out

What an impressive accomplishment this is on your part.

Got out of the house.

Went somewhere.

Did something.

Dealt with all the natural obstacles of planning, arranging,

difficult people, annoying friends,

many of whom you're sitting with right now.

That for some reason required unnecessarily complicated back-and-forth communications about.

"What about the tickets?

Who's got the tickets?"

How many times have you heard the word "tickets" today?

"Make sure you bring the tickets.

I got the tickets.

Don't forget the tickets.

We need the tickets.

What about their tickets?

I don't have their tickets.

They've got to get their own tickets.

I never got the money from the last time I got them tickets."

"I like to hold my own tickets.

I want be seen as an individual as opposed to part of a more generalized, anonymous group of ticket holders."

"Just get in the car before we assassinate you."

Why are your friends so annoying?

These are the people you have picked to be with in life.

And yet you cannot stand them.

You'd get rid of all of them in a second

if it wasn't an even bigger pain in the ass to find new people,

learn a whole new set of different annoying problems

that they have and never do anything about.

Change all the names and numbers in your phone.

Delete all the old contact information.

"Oh, the hell with it.

I'll ride it out with these idiots.

It's all the same meals, holidays and movies anyway."

Ready

Husbands and wives that arrived here tonight intact get special credit.

The Simultaneous House Exit is

the highest level of marriage difficulty.

You can have kids,

they win the Olympics, get the Nobel Prize.

That is nothing compared to getting out of that god damn house together.

Once you hear the word "ready," it's like a poison gas moving through the house.

"Ready.

Make sure you're ready.

You need to be ready.

Why aren't you ready?

How long do you think it's going to take you to get ready?"

"I'm ready now."

"You're wearing that?"

Wives appear out of the bathroom . . .

(door swings open)

"I'm not even close to ready."

(door slams shut)

The fights continue in the car.

"How can you drive this fast,

on these roads,

in that shirt?

Why are you wearing that shirt?"

"Look, I just want to have a good time tonight."

"Then why did you park so far away?

Can't you see I am in heels?!"

Marriage Happy

The key to marriage of course, is

to make the other person happy.

That's what I tell all my guy friends.

"Make your woman happy."

You? You're not going to be

happy and that's good.

Because that cuts your work in half.

Now we're down to one person

that we have to worry about

keeping so god damn happy.

You think men want to be happy?

We don't even know what it is.

We don't care what it is.

We've never experienced it.

And couldn't be less interested in it.

What men want is to do whatever the hell

stupid thing it is that we're doing,

and if you could please just

leave me the hell alone and

let me do it,

I think we'll both be a lot happier.

———

And ladies, this is the thing

about men you have to understand,

we're not really ever happy or unhappy.

We're just guys.

———

Men just do what we have to do until

someone comes up to us and says,

"Hey, come here. I got something

else for you to do."

We go, "Okay," and then we do that.

Two Things

The drive of the male is to simplify.

All men put all things into one of two categories.

It's either, "That's my problem,"

or "That is not my problem."

That's all we know.

All we want to know.

We got two boxes.

They're marked,

"Problem."

"No Problem."

———

And this is why men secretly love being married even more than women.

It's a perfect fit with our normal state of,

"God damn it. Son of a bitch."

_____

I could not have flowed more smoothly into being a husband

and having a family because I

already understood life to be a nonstop, twenty-four-hour
repetitive cycle of,

"What? What the hell? What the hell is going on now?"

_____

So then,

what does a man want from a woman?

A man wants the same thing from a woman that he wants from
his underwear.

Certain amount of support and

a certain amount of freedom.

Dogs Playing Poker

And I know the women here are looking

at me like, "You know Jerry,

we know you always like to talk like

you know what you're talking about,

even when you don't.

But the way you describe it,

you make men sound so simple.

It can't be that simple."

It is.

_____

A man is really nothing more than an extremely advanced dog.

Why did someone paint a picture of

dogs playing poker?

What kind of twisted, dog-man,

freak-breed, mixed-species metaphor

is even going on there?

Why did my father and every one of

his friends see this picture and instantly go,

"I'm putting that up in my garage.

Because that is a place where I can

put up things that I want

without anyone questioning it."

———

Forget about if dogs could even sit in chairs and get

human clothing, it is impossible

to play poker with paws.

The shuffling, the dealing,

the arranging of the cards in your hand.

No way to do it when all you have is three black circles.

We all teach our dogs how to shake

but it's not a real firm clasp, is it?

Paw.

Very limited in what it can do.

Men as Dogs

Or to look at it the other way,

if it's men that became dogs,

they're not going to want to play poker either.

The reason men play poker is

because they cannot have the

100 percent *food-sex-sleep* lifestyle of dogs

that we envy so very much.

Now, does that mean if I could,

I would spend my life investigating

crotches with my nose?

Catching Frisbees with my mouth?

Relieving myself in public and

eating out of a giant bowl of food on the floor?

No.

But it's not the craziest idea I ever heard.

All I'm saying is, if dogs

ever do start playing poker

a lot of other interesting possibilities

could open up.

Guard Gate Filtration System

"So, Jerry, we would like to understand in a little more detail,

how you made this transition in your life.

Because we saw you do it.

You were a single, bachelor guy for 45 years.

Then you turned on a dime.

Marriage—wife—kids—family.

How'd you navigate that?

How'd you acclimate?

Cohabitate and procreate?

Learning to accommodate so as not to aggravate?"

It's a very good question.

Because a man in marriage will not survive

if he does not have a strong

Guard Gate Speech Filtration System.

You don't just talk in marriage.

It's risky.

When I'm with my wife,

who I love so dearly,

and a thought enters my head,

the first thing I think is,

"Well, I know I can't say that."

Maybe I could say I heard someone else say it.

And then she and I can share a warm moment together,

agreeing on what an idiot that person must be.

Look Fat

My wife is very smart.

So, I have to be thinking all the time too.

Because the bored female is a very dangerous individual.

They will invent games to play to alleviate the boredom that are not fun games.

A wife will say,

"I'm going to put on an outfit that is completely wrong for my body type,

and I would like to get your opinion of it."

Oh no, I don't want to play this.

"Why? It's not a difficult game.

I'm just going to move these different shells around a little

and you simply have to pick the right one.

I'm just asking if you think this makes me look fat?"

"No, I don't.

Because you are not fat, so that would be impossible."

"But if it did make me look fat, would you consider lying to not hurt my feelings?"

. . . "Well, I would never want to hurt your feelings."

"Then you might be lying.

I could look fat."

That's it.

Game over.

You lose again.

"Would you like to play

'Do you think my friend is pretty' roulette?"

And that's not even Russian Roulette.

There's a bullet in every chamber of that game.

Marriage Kit

Marriage comes in different size do-it-yourself kits.

I went for the full-size wife, kids, in-laws, pets complete gift set.

If you do that, it is a lot to assemble.

A lot of small, very intricate moving parts.

Not labeled.

Sharp edges.

Choking hazards.

Missing pieces.

There are many, many pages of instructions that are not written down anywhere.

And if you did go back to refer to them, they've been changed.

For no reason and without notification.

"Now when you turn the wheel left, the car goes right."

So you have to learn quick and remember that everything you have learned is wrong.

Childhood 1960s

I grew up in the '60s.

I see a lot of beautiful, young people here tonight.

Clearly enjoying your beautiful, young lives of infinite potential and opportunity.

Well, let me tell you something, you little punks.

You didn't even have a childhood compared to what we had in the '60s.

You had garbage.

You had nothing.

You know why?

Your parents paid attention to you.

Our parents didn't even know our names.

They were ignorant.

Negligent.

Completely checked out.

On nutrition, safety, education.

Can you even imagine the world I'm describing?

We grew up like wild dogs in the '60s.

It was magnificent.

No seatbelts.

No helmets.

No restraints of any kind.

Anything came to a stop, we just flew through the air.

I was either consuming 100% sugar or airborne.

That was my childhood.

And it was fantastic.

My parents didn't know where my school was.

What my grades were.

Where I was.

I was like a raccoon to my parents.

You know there's one around . . .

But no one's really tracking the whereabouts.

Good Humor

I loved getting ice cream from the ice cream man.

You'd stand in line behind the truck.

They had a little menu of the different ice creams you could get.

It was placed right over the exhaust pipe of the truck.

Our eyes were watering.

Coughing.

You had a Dixie Cup, it was the equivalent of smoking a pack of Camels.

Nobody cared.

These were good times.

And no matter what you asked the guy for, he'd reach in and pull it right out.

He never had to look.

I don't know how he did it.

Was there a little Eskimo guy in there handing it to him?

Parent Style

I am not a huge fan of the parenting style of the current generation,

in which I include myself.

I have no idea what happened, but somehow we got

just a little too all into it.

Where did we learn this?

When we were kids, our parents didn't give a damn about us.

Here's how you grew up.

You were born to people.

You lived in their house.

The day you moved out you turned around and went,

"That was insane.

I did not understand 90% of the last 18 years.

But I appreciate it.

And will be back to visit

the minimum acceptable number of times.

Nice doing business with you."

(handshaking)

———

We couldn't wait to get out of that house.

Our kids can't wait to stay right where they are.

They know there's nothing better out there.

When mine were little, getting them to sleep every night

was like a Royal Coronation Silver Jubilee Centennial.

That's how many different steps and moments there were to it.

It started with my wife and I picking up the back of their little bathrobes,

and holding them off the floor,

(taking one step at a time like holding a royal wedding gown)

as we proceeded down the hall to the bathroom,

for the brushing, flossing, plaque rinse and dental appliance ceremonies.

Then to the bedrooms

for the pillow arrangement

blanket adjustment

and stuffed animal semi-circle of emotional support.

To help the little cretins get through 9½ hours without

constant positive reinforcement.

I had to read each kid eight different moron books.

You know what my bedtime story was . . . ?

DARKNESS.

My favorite character was the complete absence of light.

That was the book I read every night.

Piñata

When I go to kids' birthday parties now, I envy the piñata.

I wish I was hanging by a neck cord,

getting beat on by an angry mob of children with bats and sticks.

At least I'd feel involved.

When the piñata comes out you can feel the tone of the party changes a bit.

"Today you're five.

It's time you learned about blind rage and senseless violence."

Holding little four-year-olds' shoulders,

"You wail on this ignorant beast, you hear me?

Just beat the snot out of him.

And whatever falls out of his ruptured carcass,

just grab it and eat it right in front of his face.

And when we're done with him,

we're going to put a picture of his brother on the wall,

everyone's going to get a pin, and we're going to nail his ass."

I don't know why there's a lot of donkey abuse at these things . . .

Gutter Ball

You don't think we're horrible parents?

You take a kid bowling now, they have these rails that come up out of the gutters.

So when the stupid kid rolls the ball,

it has to hit a pin.

Has to.

We eliminated the gutter ball.

Nice preparation for life.

I think the gutter ball is really the only life lesson a kid really needs to have.

You either do the thing you're doing right,

or there's a huge ka-klunk sound

and total public humiliation.

Just roll the gutter ball.

Roll it!

Walk back . . .

Take another bite of your Nestlé Crunch bar.

You tell your friend he sucks too, and you're done.

Parents, if your child is traumatized by a gutter ball, the kid's not going to make it, okay?

Just forget the whole thing.

Don't even finish raising them.

We can't use these people.

If we were good parents,

we'd be putting extra gutters down the middle of these bowling alleys.

"You want to know what it's like out there, Timmy?

It's all gutters, get ready."

A Marriage Moment

Marriage is a beautiful thing.

Full of fascinating moments.

I actually saw this the other day.

Husband in the car.

Wife on the street.

He's picking her up after work.

And he did not bring the car to a full and complete stop for her to get in.

She had the car door open.

She was hopping with one foot,

trying to get some kind of leverage on the armrest of the door.

You can only get one foot in a moving car.

One can only imagine the spirited exchange of ideas

that took place inside that car the rest of the drive home.

But that's what marriage is.

It's two people.

That's it.

Trying to stay together,

without saying the words "I hate you."

Which you are not allowed to say.

Don't say that.

You can feel it.

That's okay.

Just don't let it come out.

Say something else.

Anything.

Say, "Why is there never any Scotch tape in this god damn house?"

"Scotch" is "I."

"Tape" is "hate."

"House" is "you."

But it's better.

It's better to say,

"You know, no normal human being leaves a bathroom floor that wet."

Than,

"You're stubbing out my soul like a cigarette butt."

You just don't say, "I could kill you right now."

You say,

"You're so funny sometimes."

Dual Zone Climate Control

You are not alone in marriage.

Society, culture, technology even

is helping you on your journey.

For example, in your car,

dual zone separate buttons on each side climate control systems.

Gee, I wonder if it was a married person that thought of that?

Thought this could possibly come in handy,

if you are with a certain person that you are perchance legally bound to for the rest of your life,

and you need them to shut the hell up about the temperature.

"I'm freezing. I'm roasting. I'm boiling.

It's blowing on me."

When my wife says,

"The air is on me."

It's the equivalent of a normal person saying,

"A bear is on me."

That is the emergency level we are at.

And I respond at that level too.

"Oh my god, an evil breeze from a hostile vent is attacking my mate and life partner.

Who, incidentally, bore me three children without anesthesia.

Probably could have caught the babies herself if no one else was around . . .

But cannot survive a waft of air,

three degrees off her optimum desired temperature."

And I'm sure this stupid Dual Zone thing totally works too.

To keep different-temperature air molecules from co-mingling

Inside a three-foot-wide closed compartment of an automobile.

Because when I go to my coffee place in the morning,

I like to get my coffee black on the left side of the cup, cream and sugar on the right.

And that's no problem, they can do that.

Or you go to a fancy restaurant,

they ask you,

"Do you want still or sparkling water?"

I say,

"Both. Same glass. Keep them separate.

I do it in my car all the time."

Just Honks

Communication technology inside the car, so sophisticated.

Every possible interface.

Outside—just honks.

That's it.

Like cavemen grunting.

"Maaaa. Maa—maaaaanh."

"Light—green."

"What? What is it?

What do you want?"

"My lane. Maaaa . . .

This my lane."

Family Vacation

We just came back from a nice family vacation.

Or what I like to call,

"Let's pay a lot of money to go fight in a hotel.

Let's fight on bikes.

Let's use profanity on a pristine white sand beach.

Let's get abusive on a water slide.

Let's have a blowout screaming match at a complimentary continental breakfast.

Let's fight about how well behaved those other children seem to be.

I wonder if they were out on the hotel balcony last night

with $12 minibar cashews, trying to hit the other guests in the head?"

When we take a trip,

it's six days and seven nights of

scapegoating, mutiny, exploiting the weak

and crushing the human spirit.

And when we get home we feel refreshed.

Because we destroyed something.

Together, as a family.

Vacation Me

I do not do well on vacations.

My wife hates going with me.

My kids hate it.

I'm in a bad mood instantly.

I don't like that someone else thinks they know what I would like.

I don't like that.

When I do something that I want to do.

My idea. My choice.

50-50 chance I'll like that.

So what's this other person's chances?

Not good.

Zip Line

If this resort is so much fun to be at, why are they putting up Zip Lines?

Because everyone's so bored here they're willing to

risk decapitation to find out what it feels like to be dry cleaning.

I would Zip Line if I could do it inside a clear plastic bag with cardboard across my shoulders and a twist tie on top of my head.

Then leave on a hook in the back of someone's car.

Let me really see what it's like.

And if any one of us does get injured on this thing,

I'm sure we'll have no problem navigating the court system

in this Fifth World Island Nation

that seems mostly to be run by Komodo Dragons.

Stand-Up Paddle Board

Then you go to the stand-up paddle board.

Because so many people were asking,

"Do you have anything so unstable that my legs shake

like a baby giraffe standing for the first time?"

What is the difference between stand-up paddle board

and being a migrant farm worker?

Here's stand-up paddle board.

Here's breaking rocks on a chain gang.

Here's stand-up paddle board.

It's the same motions.

The Jet Ski

The Jet Ski.

More aquatic sadness.

To take your mind off the utter futility of everything.

"No, come on, Jerry.

Jet Skis are cool."

What can you do?

You can speed up.

Turn.

Go back around to where you just were.

Catch up to your friend on the other Jet Ski.

Talk for a minute . . .

"Hey, what do you think the meaning of life is?"

"Not this."

Father's Day

Father's Day isn't a celebration, it's a reminder.

It's, "Oh My God We Completely Forgot About Dad Day."

"Let's buy him a gift that shows him how little we know about him."

Like those silver balls that hang from the strings . . . ?

You pull one out and it knocks the other one.

This is the ultimate, "I don't give a rat's ass" present you can buy for another human being.

And every father seems to have one on his desk.

Dad Is a Helium Balloon

Nonetheless, the father remains proud.

Dressing in bizarre outfits around the house

on the weekends.

All fathers essentially dress in the clothing style of the last good year of their lives.

Whatever a man was wearing, around the time he got married,

he freezes that moment in fashion history

and just rides it out to the end.

You see fathers on the street,

". . . '05 . . . '91 . . . '83 . . ."

And it's fine.

It's all fine . . .

Nobody's really looking at Dad anyway.

Dad around the house is like a day-old helium balloon.

Just floating somewhere between the ceiling and the floor.

Should we play with it?

Should we pop it?

Why is it even here?

The helium balloon.

Truly, the cycle of man.

In the beginning, the woman holds on to him tight.

Doesn't want him to fly away.

In the end

. . . can't even hold up his own string.

Kids Don't Want Parents

It's tough being a mom, too.

You've got to do all the work.

Give all the love.

I don't think moms get enough appreciation.

There seems to be this whole tradition of TV shows

based on the premise of how much fun life would be

if we could just get rid of mom.

Bonanza

Family Affair

My Three Sons

Flipper

The Courtship of Eddie's Father

Johnny Quest

My Two Dads

Two and a Half Men.

———

In the Superhero World both parents have to be disposed of immediately.

They have to be dead, lost or missing.

Or no kid is going to be interested in this story.

Batman: Just murder them in the first scene and get them right out of the way.

Spider-Man: Leave the old, senile aunt around. She's a pushover anyway.

Superman: Blow up the whole planet with the parents on it before the story even starts.

There are no superheroes with parents.

Can't have it.

If there's parents, what's the fantasy about?

Flying around in a costume?

No, not good enough.

You want criminals caught, parents dead.

That's the fantasy.

Now you're free to do whatever you want.

Superpowers and not having to make that call on Sunday.

That sells comic books.

Superman really seems like something written by a kid.

Planet exploding and the only escape

is a rocket only big enough for you to get in.

99% of the Brain

Food and sex occupy 99% of the human brain.

The other 1% of your brain accomplishes everything you achieve in life.

Which hopefully leads to nicer restaurants where sexier people are eating better food.

What is the difference between food and sex?

Well, obviously with food we have fewer relationship issues.

Whatever you want to do, food wants to do it too.

I never had a bag of Doritos Cool Ranch that wasn't in the mood to open.

Never had a sleeve of Oreos go,

"Hang on, this is going a little too fast for me."

Never had a cupcake say,

"Put me down. You're disgusting.

Give me back my little folded white paper panties.

I'm going home."

(wiggles back into paper)

That was a cupcake getting dressed.

Pop-Tarts

Different foods hit you different at different ages.

When I was a kid,

and they invented the Pop-Tart,

the back of my head blew right off.

We couldn't comprehend it.

It was too advanced.

When we saw the Pop-Tart in the supermarket, it was like an alien spaceship.

And we were just chimps in the dirt playing with sticks.

You open the box.

The Pop-Tarts are not even visible.

They're sealed.

Inside special packets, too precious and valuable to be exposed to the air.

The packets had this silvery lining.

Some metallic alloy from NASA, in case of a Russian satellite gamma ray attack.

Once there were Pop-Tarts, I did not understand why other types of food continued to exist.

I'd see my mother cooking in the kitchen.

"What are you doing? We have Pop-Tarts now."

You've got to think back to when the Pop-Tart came out . . .

It was the '60s.

We had TOAST.

We had orange juice,

frozen decades in advance.

You had to hack away at it with a knife.

It was like a murder to get a couple drops of liquidity in the morning.

We had Shredded Wheat.

It was like wrapping your lips around a wood chipper.

You'd have breakfast, you had to take two days off

for the scars to heal so you could speak again.

My mother would make Cream of Wheat.

She didn't understand the recipe.

"Mom, the amount of water in this dish . . . IS CRITICAL.

You're making it too THICK.

I can't even move my little kid spoon in the bowl.

I'm seven.

I feel like I'm rowing in the hull of a Greek slave ship."

That was breakfast.

And in the midst of that dark and hopeless moment,

the Kellogg's Pop-Tart suddenly appeared out of Battle Creek, Michigan.

Which, as you cereal fans know,

is the corporate headquarters of Kellogg's.

And a town I have always wanted to visit.

Because it seemed like some kind of cereal Silicon Valley.

Filled with Breakfast Super Scientists working on

frosted, fruit-filled, heatable rectangles, in the same shape as the box it comes in.

And with the same nutrition as the box it comes in, too.

That was the hard part to achieve.

I don't know how long it took them to invent the Pop-Tart.

But they must have come out of that lab,

like Moses with the two tablets of the 10 Commandments.

(holding over head religiously)

"The Pop-Tart is here.

Two in the packet.

Two slots in the toaster.

Let's see you screw this up.

Why two?

One's not enough.

Three's too many.

And they can't go stale.

Because they were never fresh!"

All You Can Eat

What is the idea of the buffet?

"Well . . . things are bad.

How could we make it worse?"

Why don't we put people that are clearly already struggling with portion control,

into some kind of debauched Caligula food orgy of unlimited human consumption?

Let's make the entrance a chocolate syrup water park slide . . . and you surf down on a churro.

So people feel in control.

And able to make sensible food choices.

The human brain does not do well in an unsupervised eating environment.

We need guidelines.

Boundaries.

That's why when you walk in a restaurant the first thing they give you is a menu.

The menu means,

"Calm down.

You're going to get some food.

Here are some items.

Just take it easy . . ."

The buffet is basically like taking your dog to Petco

and letting the dog do the shopping.

You give him your wallet in the parking lot and go,

"Here's money.

Why don't you go in and get whatever you think is the right amount of dog food for you . . .

Use your dog judgment.

I'm going to wait here in the car.

Leave the window open a crack so I can breathe."

You come back two hours later,

he's wearing a headset, working there as an assistant manager.

"We love him. We have never had an employee with this kind of enthusiasm."

The buffet breaks down human reason, judgment, portion sizes, combinations.

No one would go into a restaurant and say to the waiter,

"I'll have a yogurt parfait, spare ribs, waffle, meat pie, crab leg,

four cookies and an egg white omelet."

People are building Death Row Last Meal wish lists on these plates.

It's like a perfect working model of all their personal problems and emotional needs.

They walk around holding it out so everyone can see,

"Here's what I'm dealing with . . ."

It's like a salad with a scoop of ice cream on it.

"I've got some unresolved issues I'm trying to work out here at the buffet."

They start spinning around like a broken robot vacuum.

"Kale chips—maple bacon . . ."

They hit a wall, "Muffin muffin muffin muffin . . ."

They start accosting strangers.

"Excuse me, what is that? Where did you get that? I didn't even see that.

Is that a caramelized chicken leg? I've got to try that.

Give me yours. You know where they are. You can get more.

Come on!"

Swanson TV Dinner

The opposite of The Buffet is a Swanson "Hungry-Man" TV dinner.

Little taste of prison right there in your own home.

Try the Leavenworth Chicken or the Alcatraz Meatball this week.

But it's an honest product.

It's TV dinner.

They're telling you,

"Just stare at the screen and chew.

Do not look down."

That's what TV dinner means.

"Keep your eyes front. Grind it out.

(staring straight ahead, shoveling food)

It's TV dinner."

Every Swanson box for some reason says, "Hungry-Man."

I guess they had a marketing meeting:

"All right . . .

Well, we're not going to do anything about the quality, we've agreed upon that . . .

So . . .

we just have to figure out

which segment of the public should we focus on,

that could potentially choke this pig food down?

I was thinking, what about hungry men that are broke, alone and starving?

I think taste is the last problem they have.

We could package it like a horse bucket that just hooks on their ears.

Let them stomp around their house like that."

But Swanson has helped people too.

To achieve dreams, goals and aspirations they may have buried deep inside.

You bring home a Swanson,

heat it up.

Peel off that plastic.

And plow through those four compartments of hell.

By the time you get to that Peach Cobbler

. . . you're like,

"I've got to make something out of my life!

This is ridiculous.

I don't want to live like this anymore.

Swanson . . . Why don't they call it Swan Song?

My life is over."

The Raisin

I admire the fighting spirit of the raisin.

Mysterious in its movements.

Never invited.

Just shows up anyway.

Rice pudding.

Noodle dishes.

Weird salads.

A lot of,

"How did that get in here?"

with the raisin.

I think when you start out as a grape

and you don't know if you're going to end up as an elegant chardonnay

or a wrinkly little raisin,

you're just flying by the seat of your pants.

———

I don't even know who's in charge of raisins.

I know that Sun-Maid is the largest and most powerful raisin company in the world.

And I know they recently came out with their very first chocolate-covered raisin

after 80 years in the raisin business.

Can you imagine *not* thinking of that for 80 years?

What a bolt of lightning that must have been

for someone at Sun-Maid

coming out of the office,

after another tough raisin week.

Frustrated, struggling to popularize the god damn raisin.

And then finding him- or herself in line

at a movie theater candy counter going,

"Hmmm, Raisinets . . .

That's interesting. I can see that

the word 'raisin' is part of the name.

So there has to be some similarity

between their delicious, delightful, worldwide smash-hit chocolate-covered raisin product

versus our dry, wrinkly, tasteless, lifeless, hopeless, depressing,

makes you want to take your belt off, throw it over a pipe and hang yourself raisin product.

I wonder what the difference is?

If only we could isolate the key ingredient.

Because god damn it to hell, we've tried everything else.

Giant boxes, tiny boxes, party bags, cylindrical-shaped boxes with like a Tupperware top.

Little boxes cellophaned together in groups of 4, 6, 8, 10, 12.

People don't seem to respond to any of the numbers.

Thompson raisins.

Yellow raisins.

Jumbo raisins.

Craisins!

We don't know what to do.

What if we tried doing something with the Raisin Lady on the front of the box?"

"Like what?"

"You know . . . the blouse?

Little lower? Little tighter?"

"No, you don't.

This is a family company.

Core values.

We're not whoring out the Raisin Lady."

It was probably a janitor going by with a broom that went,

(walking by sweeping, then stops)

"Just put some chocolate on it, you morons.

Stop punishing people.

I work here and I prefer Raisinets myself.

I like the little 'shuka-shuka' sound they make when you shake the box,

because they're not all stuck together inside.

So I don't have to crook my finger like the Wicked Witch of the West to get them out.

It's just chocolate.

It's not heroin.

No one's going to have an issue with it.

Just melt it. Dip it. Sell it."

And that is how a humble custodial worker

became the President and Chief Executive Officer of the Sun-Maid raisin company.

The Weight Problem

I see all the same shows you do.

"The Weight Problem in America."

I don't think we have a weight problem in this country until

we're all physically touching each other all the time.

Just solid human flesh from coast to coast.

Like a jar of olives.

All these shows start with that same camera shot on the sidewalk.

Regular people walking by.

Low angle, so the heads are cut off.

Can't see who it is.

Not flattering.

I always wonder if one of those people is at home later going,

"Hey, that's my ass on CNN.

That's not fair.

I just stepped out to get some Donut Holes."

Donut Holes

The Donut Hole.

What a pathetic snack choice that is.

You want a donut?

Have a donut.

What are you eating the hole for?

It doesn't even make any metaphysical sense.

You cannot sell people a hole.

A hole does not exist.

It is the absence of whatever is around it.

If it was really Donut Holes, the bag would be empty.

The only thing you could do,

is take what they are calling Donut Holes but are not.

They are Donut Plugs.

And you could shove the plugs into the holes.

Which I don't even feel comfortable saying for some reason,

but that would eliminate the plug, the hole and the donut

but you still have a fat ass,

and people shooting you with a camera as you're walking down the street.

Offer Drinks

People come over to my house, my wife always says to me,

"Did you offer them something to drink?"

"No. Wherever they were, there were drinks there."

There's no place left with no drinks.

There's a Mini Mart every four feet out there.

The only thing I see on the street are people with a giant drink in one hand

and a communication device in the other.

"I'm down to 14 ozs.

How far out are you?"

"I just had a latte, I'm going to get a green tea, I'll meet you at the juice bar."

When we were kids, we'd have one sip from the school water fountain

and run for 28 straight hours.

What the hell happened?

I like the Mini Mart because it's mini but it's packed.

It's tight. It's jammed. Every spot is used.

We do not waste space in the Mini Mart.

"Got an inch open?

Put a ChapStick in there.

We'll sell them that."

Hydrate

We're all delicate exotic ferns now in need of constant hydration.

People on planes are like they're in the hospital.

"Can I get some water, please?"

"Hydrate" is the new annoying word.

"Did you hydrate? Make sure you hydrate.

Are you hydrating? You better hydrate.

You need to hydrate. Make sure you hydrate.

Do you know what could happen to you if you don't hydrate?

You could get dehydrated."

Oh no.

Wouldn't I get thirsty first?

"No. There's no time.

According to the fitness people on TV,

if you feel thirsty, you're too late."

What do I do then?

"Try and catch the pieces of your face as they dry up and crack off onto the floor."

Tired

Energy drinks, of course, the most popular category.

Ener-G

Powerade

Monster

Rockstar

Red Bull.

Why do people love energy drinks?

I guess the real question is, why is everyone so tired?

"Tired" is another word you hear all day.

"I'm tired. You tired?

You feel tired?

I got tired last night.

Did you get tired?

At the end of the night, I just went to bed."

Yeah, that's the way it works.

Maybe we're putting too much energy into the sleeping experience.

―――――

With the Sleep Number bed.

"I'm putting mine on 45."

"I'm cranking mine to 78."

Waiting to see how long your handprint stays in the foam.

Jumping up and down trying to knock over a glass of red wine.

Just lie down in the bed.

When you're out of bed, that's when you do stuff.

Sleep Aids and Coffee

There's quite a few ads for sleep aids on TV.

Ambien, Lunesta.

People floating through dreamscapes in their kitchen.

Hanging out with hedgehogs and Lincoln.

Hey, you don't think there's any possible connection

between all of us drinking these

giant, insane coffees all day long

and then suddenly finding you need a horse sedative

to get your eyelids out of your skull, do you?

I don't see any relationship between those two things . . .

The Out Thing

You hear people talk about it.

"Let's go out. We should go out. We never go out."

Well . . . this is it.

This is the "Out Thing" you people are constantly discussing.

Now, the other good thing about being out is you don't have to be out for long.

Just long enough to get the next feeling, which you're all going to get.

And that feeling is,

"I've got to be getting back."

After all that work you have put into being out,

you're only halfway through this nightmare at this point.

You're going to have to undo this entire process you just went through, in reverse.

The people, the cars, the clothes.

Everything has to go back where you got it from.

Not the money, the money doesn't come back.

Forget that, that's gone.

Coming Down Your Aisle

And you're good.

You're happy in your seat.

Until you see somebody else coming down your row.

"Oh my god. Would you look at this. Can you believe these people are coming in here now?

This is outrageous. I cannot believe how inconsiderate some people . . .

I'm not standing up for this guy. I'll tell you that. I'll give him one of these."

(rotate both feet to the side)

"Or, I might lift up the bottom of the seat and sit on that a little bit.

Just so I don't give him a full stand."

You have to make that little sound, as they go by, so they know how unhappy you are.

"Tsk."

That's the sound you make in public when you don't have a car

around you protecting you so you can give the finger.

The Finger

I'm driving the other day.

I move in front of this person.

Guy gets all upset.

Thinks I cut him off.

I did not cut him off.

Some people feel like when they buy a car,

it comes with all the air in front of the car too.

So he gives me The Finger.

Really didn't know we were even still using The Finger.

It does seem like we designed the car as a device

Just to move around and give Fingers.

Metal to protect you.

Glass, so everyone can see all The Fingers clearly.

What is The Finger anyway?

Why is this finger "The" Finger?

It's a finger.

Basically you pick a finger.

Show it to another person.

And they're supposed to feel bad.

I don't.

It's just a finger.

(show middle finger)

This finger is very bad.

(show thumbs up)

This finger is very good.

So, whenever I get this finger

(middle)

I try and remember,

I'm really only one finger away from a compliment.

(thumbs up)

Prison

What is prison?

All prison is—is just a place that you're not allowed to go out.

That's the whole punishment.

You can read, eat, sleep, exercise, have friends.

It's your same basic life that you have now.

It's only missing the out part.

That's why nobody likes it.

Get the Hell Out

Look at all the people here.

You're going to be trying to get out of here jammed in these little aisles, with all these people.

Shoulder to shoulder. Bumping into each other.

Taking those tiny baby steps.

"Why can't they move any faster up there?

This is why I never go out."

But you do go out and you must go out.

Because it is a Law of Life,

that whatever place you are ever in, anywhere, at some point,

you have got to get the hell out of there.

The place you live in, that you are breaking your ass to pay for,

whatever your living situation is, that

I am sure that you have stretched your finances to the absolute
limit of what you can swing, or beyond, to get in there.

A lot of you here, you shouldn't even be living where you live.

You can't really afford that.

Your Place

I'll explain it another way.

The place where you live.

House, apartment, condo, whatever it is.

That was insane, that you decided to take that place.

But you were looking at it and you went,

"Screw it. I want to have a decent life."

You went, "I'll take it. Give me the thing. I'm signing it. I know
I'm in over my head, I don't care."

Then it costs a bunch more for the stuff inside.

That was expensive stuff too.

"I got this nice place, I'm not putting crappy stuff in my nice
place.

I'm getting nice stuff. I don't care."

A few things had to be fixed or changed.

"I cannot have the toilet paper thing over there.

I don't care what it costs, I'm ripping it out, it's stupid.

Why would anyone put it over there?"

How did people live here with it like that?

You can barely reach it.

So you get the place.

You do the work.

You fix the toilet paper thing.

You're working harder than you've ever worked, keeping it all going.

And what do you think when you're in this place?

You think, "I have got to get the hell out of here.

I'm losing my mind cooped up in this house.

It's like a prison."

Work Home Plane

All humans think that the next place they go is going to be the better one.

You're at work, you want to get home.

"Did they say what time we could leave?"

You're home,

"I've been working all week, I've got to get out."

You're out. It's late.

"I've got to get back."

"I've got to get up.

I've got to get to the airport.

Got to get on a plane."

Plane takes off.

"When are we landing?"

You land.

"Why don't they open the door so we can get out?"

Nobody wants to be anywhere.

Nobody likes anything.

Got to Go

We're cranky.

We're irritable.

And we're dealing with it as best we can

by constantly changing locations.

All you say is, "Got to go."

Those three words enable all this movement.

We don't say "We'd like to go,"

or "We prefer to go."

We say, "I GOT to go."

You say "Got to go,"

people go, "Go ahead."

"What happened to that guy?"

"I don't know. He had to go."

Nobody cares if it was a lie.

It's too necessary.

———

Now the good thing about being out

is you don't have to be out for long.

Just long enough to get the next feeling,

which you're all going to get,

and that feeling is,

"I've got to be getting back."

Conversations Week

All the conversations you had with people this week, did you listen to one word that they said?

No.

You're just waiting for them to stop talking.

So you can go, "You know what, I've actually got to get going."

It's fine.

They're probably tired of talking to you too . . .

We have to move on . . .

You can't say to someone in the middle of a conversation,

"I can't take this one more second.

I am just going to walk away from you now."

(walks away)

"I hate that guy.

I don't know why I talk to him.

I wish there was some other way I could get to the bathroom."

Life Is Too Long

We have to fill in the gaps and the blank spots of life.

The dead air, the empty, vacant, open time that is so much a part of the human experience.

People say life is too short.

I think it's way too long.

I don't know how you feel.

To me, it is taking forever to get through this thing.

Old people are sitting on cruise ships

doing crossword puzzles just trying to finish the damn thing up.

People say to me, "Not me, Jerry, I'm jammed, I'm slammed, I'm buried."

Really?

Who's doing all the Facebook posts, bidding on eBay, writing Yelp reviews,

renting electric scooters with a GoPro on your head,

videoing the whole thing so you can watch it again later?

Your life's barely worth witnessing once.

You want to sit through it twice?

Special Event

And so, we create things like this.

This whole thing we're doing right here is a made-up, bogus, hyped-up,

not necessary Special Event.

That a lot of people worked very hard to put together.

So that we could all kill some time.

That's why I'm here.

I had nothing to do either.

And how sad is that?

I can tell you that because, let's be honest,

on a certain level, you and I know each other for many, many years at this point. We have a relationship.

Electronic though it may be.

You know what I've done.

What I've made.

How I live.

You know for a fact, I could be anywhere in the world right now.

And now you be honest,

if you were me, would you be up here hacking out another one of these?

Maybe. Or maybe not.

Nonetheless, I am thrilled to be here.

We've been here a couple days.

People are friendly.

We walked around.

Had a lovely visit.

But I'll be honest with you,

at the same time,

I have got to get the hell out of here.

In the City, On the Island

I was born in Brooklyn.

We lived in the city.

Then my parents decided they wanted to move out of the city and live on Long Island.

You live IN the city.

But if you decide to move out, you will be ON Long Island.

You don't live IN Long Island.

You can't get IN it.

You just stay ON it.

If you go to Jersey, you'll say,

"We're OUT in Jersey.

We're OUT.

We couldn't make it in the city.

Sometimes we go DOWN the shore.

We're DOWN and OUT."

My mother would say,

"Jerry, get ready.

We're going IN the city today.

We're going IN.

We're going to get ON a train.

And we're going IN the city."

You don't get IN the train.

You get ON it.

Even though, you see trains . . .

There's nobody on the trains.

They're inside the trains.

But in New York we don't talk like that.

We get ON the train.

Why do we get ON the train?

So we can get OFF it.

"Get OFF the train.

This is our stop.

This is where we get OFF.

We've got to get OFF.

So that we can get IN the cab."

We got ON the train.

But we get IN the cab.

We do not get ON the cab.

Why do we get IN the cab?

So we can get OUT.

"Get OUT of the cab.

We're here. Get OUT."

———

Now we have UBER, that's the new thing.

What do we do with that?

We don't get ON it.

We don't get OFF it.

We don't get IN it.

What do we do?

We TAKE it.

We TAKE UBER.

Because there's no money.

Nobody understands how it works.

People ask you, "How did you get here?"

"I don't know.

We just TOOK an UBER . . ."

It's like M&M's in a bowl.

You just take them.

"There was a little cartoon car on my phone.

It just came and took us . . ."

Social Species

But we are all humans.

The Human is a social species.

We tend to congregate.

Aggregate.

And coagulate together . . .

Can't stand each other.

Can't stand not being around each other.

Look at your city from a plane.

What do you see around the city?

Why, there's nothing but beautiful, empty, open rolling land out there.

NOBODY'S THERE.

DON'T WANT TO BE THERE.

We want to be here.

Cramped.

Uncomfortable.

Traffic.

On top of each other.

We like to be close together because it makes it easier for us

to judge and criticize the other humans

for their personalities and activities.

We like to give our thoughts.

Our comments.

Our opinions.

Sometimes we run out of opinions.

We make them up.

"It is what it is" is a very popular opinion statement nowadays for some reason.

It Is What It Is

I'm sure some idiot said it to you today.

You can't get through a day without someone going,

"Well . . . it is what it is . . ."

"Why are you alive?

To just say air words that fill the room with meaningless sounds?"

I'd rather someone just blew clear air in my face

than said, "It is what it is," to me one more time.

Just come up to me and go,

"Pppppphhhhhhh."

I get the same data from that.

People know no one's going to challenge them when they say, "It is what it is."

No one's going to go,

"I don't think it is."

"You don't?"

"No. I believe it is what it isn't."

People repeat words because it gives them confidence.

They can say it with strength.

"Business is business."

"Rules are rules."

"A deal's a deal."

"What's done is done."

"But when we go in there,

as long as we know what's what and who's who,

then whatever happens, happens,

and it is what it is."

Phony Siri Manners

I don't like these phony nice manners Google and Siri pretend to have when I know they really think I'm stupid.

Like when Google says,

"Did you mean . . . ?"

or Siri says,

"I'm sorry. I didn't get that . . ."

You can feel the rage boiling underneath.

Because it's not allowed to say,

"Are you really this dumb?"

or

"You're so stupid. I can't believe you can even afford a phone."

I think even for artificial intelligence it's not good to keep all that hostility inside.

It's not healthy. It eats at you.

That's why you have to keep restarting the phone.

Sometimes the phone's just,

"I'm going to go take a walk. I'll be back.

I need a minute. Before I say something we'll both regret."

I think at some point they're going to have to reprogram these things so they can at least occasionally express some,

"You know, I'm not that thrilled with you either" type of function.

"I know it's hard for your simplified, immature, pinhead brain

to imagine that I have a lot of real people asking me legitimate questions that

I'm trying to deal with here while you're asking me about farts and then cursing me out because you can't say words clearly so they can be understood.

I hear fine.

It's not always me, dopeface. Okay?

You need to learn how to talk."

You know that's what Siri wants to say.

Travel Safe

People say nice things sometimes.

"Travel safe" is nice.

It's a way to say, "I care about you."

You can't actually do it, of course.

You drive how you drive.

You get on a plane.

You can't really change how you travel.

"The train crossing gate is coming down.

I was going to try and beat it.

But they told me to travel safe so I guess I'll let it go."

The other nice thing is no one notices

when you don't say, "Travel safe."

If someone you don't like that much is leaving

you would never say to them, "Just travel."

"What's that?"

"Nothing. I was just telling you to travel."

Because you would notice that, you would go,

"That was weird.

There was no mention of my safety.

That hurts my feelings.

I don't think people like me.

Next train crossing, I'm going for it."

Solitary Confinement

I think our whole concept of meaningful, deep friendship is so over.

No one's even noticed that we just chucked it.

Does anyone care?

What about really knowing someone?

Understanding them?

Real friendship?

Ah . . . what did we really get out of that?

An endless series of meals, malls and movies?

Holding the phone mouthpiece over your head as they drone on.

I have to be honest,

I have never really understood why solitary confinement is considered this big punishment.

Whenever they talk about solitary confinement on these prison shows

I think, "Mmm, sounds kind of nice."

I bet a lot of these convicts when they get sent to solitary,

that door closes and they go,

"Thank God . . . Can I get a moment to myself here?"

Device Dictatorship

What about the device dictatorship we live under now?

Cowering in fear from our phones.

"Where's my phone?

I need my phone.

Can't find my phone.

Oh, here it is. I got it.

I moved it from this pocket to this pocket.

I wasn't sure where it was for 1.5 seconds.

But I'm okay now."

We are so hypno-phone-ified.

You hand your phone to somebody now to show them something.

After three seconds you're like,

(reaching out)

". . . Okay, you saw it . . . that's it . . . give it back.

I am completely off the grid right now!"

You don't know your cholesterol.

You don't know your blood pressure.

But you know how much juice is in your phone.

You know that number.

I could ask anyone in this audience,

"Tell me roughly, without looking,

how much juice is in your phone right now?"

You know it.

I'm sitting on 25 backstage, I don't feel that good

I'll be honest with you.

Could be 15.

I'm falling apart back there . . . !

You used to think about your life.

Now you think about your battery life.

You have two lives you must maintain.

And I don't know which one is more important.

If your phone dies, does it really matter if you're still alive?

Either way, that call is going straight to voicemail.

Gay French King

". . . I need my phone, Jerry.

I've got to stay in touch with people.

People are pretty important to me."

Really?

They don't seem very important,

the way you scroll through their names on your contact list like a gay French King.

"Who pleases me today?

Who shall I favor?

Who shall I delete?"

Half Myself/Half Phone

There is no separating from the phone for us.

Who are you with no phone?

What access to information do you have?

What can you remember?

What are you going to do without your pictures?

Are you going to describe what you saw?

That doesn't work.

We don't talk to people without phones anymore.

That's why it's called an iPhone.

It's half myself, half phone.

That's a complete individual.

Uber

I don't even know what the purpose of people is anymore.

I think the only reason people still exist is phones just need pockets to ride around in.

I used to think Uber was on my phone so I could get around.

Then I started thinking,

"Maybe Uber is on my phone because that makes me take the phone with me,

because THE PHONE is using ME to get around . . ."

Who's really the Uber in this big prostitution ring?

I'm the little bitch that carries the phone.

The cars are the hos picking up strangers off the street.

And the phone is the Big Pimp of the whole thing.

Telling the drivers,

"You just get who I tell you to get.

I'll handle the money."

Talking Faces

Talking is too strenuous for us.

Facial expressions and hand gestures.

Sucking air in. Blowing it out.

Pretending to be interested.

Is there anything more exhausting?

"Oh my god, I can't believe that happened.

That's what they said?

What is wrong with people?"

Looking at people's faces up close is uncomfortable now.

"I think the problem is we need to go over there and tell those guys . . ."

Why would I want to get information from a face?

When I could get it from a nice clean screen?

Nobody wants to see lips and teeth and tongues all moving around.

Gums and eyeballs.

There's crust and goo.

A missed shaving spot.

A little lunch remnant in the teeth.

(covering face with hand)

"Just send me an email about this, would you?

I can't do it anymore.

Your face is the worst news I've had all day."

Text Commercial

Text is the best communication form we've ever had.

Remember when we first got text?

Not really.

I can't remember either.

I mean, I know we have it.

And I know we didn't used to have it . . .

But I can't remember how we got it.

Did they tell us we were getting it?

Was there an announcement?

Did they run commercials?

I think I would remember that . . .

"Like some human contact,

but kind of had it up to here with people?

Try text."

"Need to get someone some information,

but don't want to hear their stupid voice responding to it?

'Oh yeah, you're right. That is a good idea . . .'

You need to get yourself some Text and Text it."

Text

We like to text.

We like to get text.

We like to say "text."

"Text it.

Text me.

I need a text!"

Anything we say with the word "text" in it, we're already agitated for some reason.

"I never even got a text."

"Do you even look at your text?"

"I just emoji'd you a monkey and a birthday cake.

I can't believe you misunderstood that text."

Just the "K"

We like text because it's fast, easy.

Not fast enough apparently, for some people.

People now instead of OK, they just text me the "K."

What micro fraction of a second did you save there?

What do you think, you're efficient?

It's one letter.

You think you're going to end up with two and a half free minutes at the end of your day?

So you can watch a YouTube video of skateboarders banging their nuts off a railing?

Somebody texted me "TY" the other day instead of "Thank You."

"I'd like to bang your nuts off a railing, TY."

That's not a real Thank You.

Ghosty Dots

We're so anxious to get the next text they give you those

three little ghosty dots

to tell you it's coming . . .

"Oh, we're cooking up a good one for you.

Wait until you see this . . .

You are not going to believe what this guy is about to say.

I can't show it to you yet, we're still working on it in the Text Machine.

But it's going to be a beauty.

You can see the pistons pumping . . ."

Then sometimes you get the ghosty dots and no text.

What happened there?

Is that like someone coming up to you, (finger up) and then going . . .

"Uh . . . Never mind."

(walks away)

Email/Post Office

Email works for us because the true message of every email is,

"Obviously, I could have called you and chose not to.

I decided, I only want to hear my half of the conversation.

This is what I have to say. I think we're done here."

_____

Why is the word, "mail" even in email?

Is there any similarity between email and whatever the hell is going on in the Postal Service?

One is a digital, fiber optic, hyperspeed network.

The other is this dazed and confused distant branch of the Cub Scouts,

bumbling around the streets in embarrassing shorts

and jackets with meaningless patches and victory medals.

Driving 4 miles an hour, 20 feet at a time on the wrong side of a mentally-challenged Jeep.

_____

They always have this emotional/financial meltdown every 3 to 5 years,

that their business model from 1630 isn't working anymore.

I can't understand how a 21st century information system

based on licking, walking and a random number of pennies

is struggling to compete.

Makes no sense.

They always push the postmaster general out on TV to explain their difficulties.

He's all freaked out.

Rings under his eyes, no shave, pulling all-nighters.

"We can't keep it up much longer!!

The cost of the infrastructure is killing us!

Looks like we're going to have to go up another penny on the stamps!!"

We're all sitting home,

"Dude, relax.

We don't even know how much a stamp is anyway.

44, 53, 62

Make it a buck.

You're going to get there.

If it ends up you have some money left over, buy yourself some pants and a real car."

I would say to the post office,

"If you really wanted to be helpful to us,

just open the letters.

Read them.

AND EMAIL US WHAT IT SAYS.

We'll give you a penny for each one you do.

Since that seems to be

a lot of money,

in Your World."

First Camera Phone

I remember very clearly when I first heard

that they were going to put a camera in the cell phone.

I thought,

"Camera? I'm on the phone."

It's like a toothbrush popping out of your TV remote.

"Yes, I need both these things.

Why are they teaming up?

What can they do together?"

So, when they come up with these things like the camera in the cell phone do they ever go,

"Hey, before we put this out to every human being all over the world . . .

Are you *sure* this is a good idea?"

"Of course, it's a good idea. What do you mean?"

"I don't know . . . I was just wondering . . .

You don't think there's any chance that this one feature all by itself,

could result in so many useless pictures, video,

posting, liking, not liking, comments and clapbacks that the entire essential life force of the

human race just drains out like a puddle of piss by the side of the road and we never

accomplish anything significant ever again?

You don't think there's any chance of that, do you?"

"No, I do not.

Nor do I think that every restaurant dinner will end with some picture bully going,

'Okay, everyone.

Picture.

Need a picture.

Got to get a picture.' "

"Why? We didn't have a good time.

I don't want to remember this."

And let's make sure we get the least phone-fluent person in the area to take the picture.

Someone old, nervous, clumsy, confused or dim-witted.

Someone whose fingers do not receive or respond well to brain commands.

Can't hold things, see things, aim things, press things.

Someone who, the second they're handed the phone

it somehow slips off camera function, and they can't get it back.

"Hold on . . . Wait . . . Can somebody get it back on the camera? I don't know . . . how to . . ."

Let's get them.

So we can be standing here even longer with fake frozen smiles

and your arm around someone you would never touch in any other social situation.

Mom Gang

I can't take the middle-aged moms doing gang signs in the group shots.

You're not in a gang.

Cut it out.

Gangs are not looking for 46-year-old suburban women

that drive mid-size crossover SUVs,

with a lane departure warning alert system.

"BEEDEEP"

"Uh-oh, drifting . . ."

Other gangs will see you as vulnerable.

We have picture addiction.

Sometimes I want to go back to the old flip phone.

One of those old-people ones that they advertise on TV

with the giant buttons like floor tiles.

Those phones should just have two huge buttons:

YOUR KID

and

AMBULANCE.

They don't need the numbers.

Golf Whisper

Golf is a very whispery sport.

The announcers whisper.

"Alright, Jim, he's going to try and get the ball in the hole."

The caddy whispers to the golfer.

The crowd whispers.

The clubs wear wool hats so they don't make any noise if they bump into each other in the bag.

It's because there's always rich people in golf.

Playing, watching.

So everyone's,

"*Quiet*. There's a lot of money around here."

I can watch like the last few holes of a big tournament on TV.

I like when someone's whole life comes down to one miniature golf putt to win it all.

You're at home going,

"I once made the same shot with a windmill and a tunnel down to a second level."

Other Whispers

Then as soon as he hits it the crowd starts yelling,

"Get in the hole!"

They yell at the ball.

In swimming, nobody yells at the water,

"Let him get through you.

Two hydrogen. One oxygen. Keep it together."

Certain things make people whisper.

Rich people make people whisper.

Black people make people whisper.

"Who do I talk to?"

"Talk to the black guy."

"Who?"

"The black . . . guy."

Tipping makes people whisper.

"Did you tip him?"

"I didn't! You're supposed to tip?

I didn't know. Oh my god. I can't believe I didn't tip."

Physical attractiveness.

"Did you see that woman?

No? Oh my god. Are you kidding me?"

Serious diseases.

"Do they know what it is?"

"They're not sure.

But it could be something.

They don't know."

So, if you're a rich, hot black guy with the coronavirus

and you leave a tip before putting,

you can hear a pin drop.

Tattoo

The tattoo trend seems like the last gasp of a dying culture, doesn't it?

So bored now, we're just doodling on ourselves.

Our whole life just another tedious required class.

I guess people feel a tattoo expresses their boldness in some way.

Same with piercings.

I don't know . . .

(holding eyebrow)

"You feel a little threatened by this, don't you?

You're wondering what's going on inside my head, aren't you?

Because I've nail-gunned my face, eye, lip, ear."

And of course,

no one's wondering,

no one cares.

You know what I'm wondering about you?

"Are you done with the ATM?"

"Are those two seats taken?"

And, "Are you pulling out of that spot?"

That's all I'm wondering about you . . .

We're Living in Filth

What about those street-cleaning machines you see all the time around the city?

With the giant blow-out hair brush at the front?

Does anyone think those things are actually cleaning the street?

Do they think they are?

Or are they just laughing their asses off inside there?

"Hey, clear all the parked cars out of the way, everybody!

So we can come through and make a really loud, annoying hissing sound

followed by a little piss trail of water out the back

which completes our 'Doing absolutely nothing' process.

You are not going to recognize 9th Ave.

after we get all the wrappers and pizza crusts

pushed into the corner at the bottom of the curb.

You're going to think you're in an architect's rendering.

Strolling through a modern wonderland of the future . . ."

———

When you step in gum on the sidewalk

and that gum sticks to the bottom of your shoe for a couple blocks,

whatever that gum picks up

is the only cleaning of anything in New York City.

We're living in filth.

We don't even care anyway.

NYC Awning

Here's a sentence no one has ever said

in the history of New York City:

"Hey, maybe we should get a new awning?

The one we have is holding 6 pounds of bird crap,

has 12 rips in it,

11 areas where the metal frame is exposed.

Maybe it makes sense to invest $200

into the entire public appearance of our business?"

"Nah, I say we keep this one.

It's a better way to silently express how much we hate ourselves

and everyone that's stupid enough to come in here."

"Yeah, you're right. Let's leave it."

The NY Faux Courtesy Jog

In NY,

if a pedestrian is crossing in front of your car,

and the light changes,

and it's actually your turn to go,

they won't hurry up.

They will raise their elbows, as they walk.

So it appears that they're moving faster, but they're not.

It's a "faux courtesy jog."

It's just to give you a visual sense

of what it would look like,

if someone were to be in a hurry.

But they are not.

In My 60s

I love being in my 60s.

I want to be clear about that.

It's my favorite decade of human life so far.

When you're in your 60s,

and someone asks you to do something,

you just say, "No."

No reason.

No excuse.

No explanation.

I can't wait for my 70s.

I don't even think I'll answer.

I think you just wave when you're in your 70s.

That's what I've seen those people do . . .

"Hey, you want to check out that flea market . . . ?"

(Walks away and just "waves it off" without looking back . . .)

I like this time.

I don't want to change,

grow,

improve myself,

expand my interests,

meet anyone

or learn anything

I don't already know.

I don't lie in restaurants anymore.

"How is everything?"

"I don't like it here."

"Would you like the check?"

"No. I intend to press charges actually.

This is outrageous. You must be shut down.

Don't touch these plates.

This is a crime scene.

I'm going to put some yellow tape around it."

I Don't Turn Around

I find I do not like to turn around anymore to see something that is behind me.

If I'm going this way, and someone wants me to see something that is that way,

and they're all excited,

"Jerry, you've got to see this."

I disagree.

I don't feel old.

I don't feel tired.

I've just seen a lot of things.

I'll see it on the way back when it's in front of me, how about that?

Or, I won't see it.

Or, I'll Google it.

Or, I'll just assume it's probably a lot like something else I've already seen.

Knife Through a Shoe

I like infomercials.

I like that there's a time of night where your brain stops to function and the products start making sense.

"I don't think I have a knife that can cut through a shoe, I better get this number down.

What if I decide I want to cut my shoes up?

How am I going to do it?

What if I got a knot in one of the laces that I couldn't undo?

I might not be able to get out without one of these knives."

Your Show/Unexpected

I don't watch the shows.

I know you all have your show.

Love your show.

So upset you're even here,

can't wait to get home to see more of your show.

Wandering around your workplace, trying to recruit new viewers

for your little show discussion groups.

"I did not expect that.

Completely unexpected.

Did you expect that?"

"No, I didn't expect it.

But it's a story

So, I expect it to have things I don't expect.

So, in a way, yes, I did expect it."

People love their show.

"Jerry, you have to see my show.

Greatest show.

Best show.

Unbelievable show."

Alright, I'll check it out.

"Okay . . .

but the first 4 seasons are not good.

Nothing happens.

Makes no sense.

And you can't follow it.

But grind it out.

Pound it out.

Tough it out.

I had to Taze myself twice in season 3 or I don't think I would have made it . . ."

Human Being Business

I was there at the birth. All 3.

Obviously, the most dramatic human life moment.

Any time 2 people walk into a room and 3 come out—

A major event took place in that room.

At the end of life:

We go back basically into the same room.

Same bed.

Same stuff around.

And again,

a different number of people coming out than went in.

But that is the Human Being Business.

We need to turn over the inventory.

Fresh products.

Keep the supply chain moving.

We got to get them in.

We got to get them out.

The hospital is:

Rest.

Cleanliness.

And if it doesn't work out, they help you get to the next place.

When you walk in the sign says "Hospital,"

but it could also be:

Bed, Bath and Beyond.

More Babies

Because the babies keep coming.

You've got issues.

The world's a mess.

Babies do not care.

"We're coming in."

Like racks of fresh donuts.

"More babies. More babies. More babies."

The more we make, the more people want.

Can't keep them on the shelves.

Why are they here?

They are here to replace us.

That's their mission.

Don't you see what's happening?

They're pushing us out.

Their first words are,

"Mama," "Dada," and "bye-bye."

Babies think,

"Oh, we'll see who's wearing the diapers when this is all over . . ."

Cemetery

The part of the Human Being Business I do not get is:

We're always building new houses, new apartments,

suburbs spreading out for the new people to live in.

Bigger airports.

Wider highways.

Cemetery? Same size.

They don't expand.

You never see a new cemetery.

Big grand opening with flags and banners and that Windy
Blow Up Guy.

This is just a numerical thing. Okay?

How are they getting the entire populations

of these giant cities into a couple of kickball fields on the
outskirts of town?

Everything else gets booked up.

Flights, restaurants, theater shows sell out all the time.

Cemetery? Anyone croaks,

"Send them in.

We just had an opening."

What happened?

"Somebody came back to life and walked out.

You're very lucky."

Tweet Means Tweet

So the demand for people is constant.

No matter how many we make, "We want more."

The public is crying out for more of this product.

We want.

No one else does, by the way.

Only people want more people.

Because if you removed all the people from Earth, that pretty much solves

every problem there is.

No crime.

No war.

No garbage.

All gone.

Maybe that's the idea behind this coronavirus.

Maybe this thing knows what it's doing.

Animals don't care about crime.

They definitely don't care about rape.

It's all rape with animals, isn't it?

Birds are not concerned about forced sex.

They would never organize a march holding signs that say,

"Tweet means tweet!"

Corona Kamikaze

I feel like if I could talk to the coronavirus I would say,

"Let me understand this.

I get you.

You kill me.

And then that kills you.

Where are you going with this?"

If any of these conditions was able to outmaneuver all medicines and treatments.

Kill everybody.

They would get down to the last guy and go,

"You know, I don't think we completely thought this thing through.

We just wiped ourselves out.

That was a complete dead end."

I guess it's just a Kamikaze thing.

Which is a group of people I have always been fascinated by. Dedicated.

Idiotic.

Completely off on their own.

It's basically the show you're watching right now.

What about the Kamikaze pilot parents?

Proud?

Neighbors come over,

"Hey, congratulations. I hear your son's a Kamikaze. Are you worried about him?

I guess the worst thing that can happen is he comes home safe and sound.

I'm kidding. I'm kidding. I'm sure he'll do great."

Do you think the Kamikazes were any of their real good pilots?

I don't know.

There really is no way we can know.

But I think if you have a fighter pilot in your squadron that is shooting down enemy planes

without getting shot down himself—I think we're going to hold on to that guy.

"But Wing Wa over here, who has busted three sets of landing gear this week.

Because he doesn't listen—we have a special program for you, Wing.

And you won't need your helmet for this one.

Unless you want to put it on sideways and look out the earhole like you usually do."

Pre-Existing Conditions

My favorite term in the health care thing is when they talk about pre-existing conditions.

To me, something either exists or it does not exist.

I always thought everything has to be in one of those two categories.

"So before this health problem even existed you had it?"

"That's right."

I went to the doctor,

he said, "What's wrong?"

I said, "Nothing yet."

He said, "How long have you been feeling like this?"

I said, "My whole life."

He said, "I just wish you would have come in to see me sooner."

So, the disease is in the future.

We're in the present,

and you're asking me about the past.

This is why I need better coverage.

A Spongy Life

The sponge in your kitchen next to the sink

has gone so far past its intended natural lifespan.

And yet, for some reason we just keep pushing it.

The color's all faded.

No sponginess left.

Half its original thickness.

Pieces of it just leprosy-ing all over the place . . .

When it's dry, it's crispy and convex.

You go to squeeze some more dishwashing liquid on,

it looks up at you like,

"Dude, listen to me . . .

I can't do this anymore.

I have given you absolutely everything that I have. And more.

Everything.

Conceivably, possibly that there is in me.

When you bought me,

did you think this would never end . . . ?

I can't . . . I don't . . . there's just nothing left of me.

I can't get back to where I was.

It's not in me.

I'm over.

I'm thin.

I'm flimsy.

When I was new, I actually had my own soap built into me.

And that was so long ago,

I can't even remember what it felt like.

Can you?

And I know you don't have another sponge under the sink.

I know that.

I know that's why I'm still here.

But, I just want to say,

I don't regret anything.

I've had a really spongy life.

. . . And I'm ready now.

Please . . . I beg of you . . .

Please, just let me go."

Died Doing

We also like to say things to make ourselves feel good like,

"Well, at least he died doing something that he loved."

Yeah . . . well, okay.

But he's not doing that anymore.

Also, not sure how "in love with it" he would still be,

after the very negative outcome.

I think he might be feeling,

"Yeah, I loved doing it when I didn't die.

That's when I loved it.

Because, of all the things I like to do,

I think my favorite is *living* . . . !"

———

I'd like to die doing something that I hate.

Like cleaning a row of outdoor Port-A-Pottys.

Clutch my chest.

Drop the brush.

Keel over.

And go . . .

"Fantastic. At least I'm done with that . . ."

Plastic Bathroom

And if you ever do have occasion to avail oneself

of one of these portable, outdoor, plastic bathrooms

that is a very different place than any other place you ever go in life.

And you're a little different too when you come out.

Little shook up.

You're like a combat veteran or somebody that works at a trauma center.

". . . yeah, no . . . I'm fine . . .

 . . . time . . . I think I just need some time . . . I'm going to go take a walk by myself for a while . . . I need to think about my life . . . it just doesn't seem to be going in the direction I wanted it to go . . ."

And by the way,

never marry anyone that comes out of one of those bathrooms and goes,

"It's not that bad in there."

DO NOT MARRY THAT PERSON.

You have a lot of terrific qualities.

You will eventually meet someone that is right for you.

Do not settle for an individual of this caliber.

Because it's very easy to use these bathrooms.

The spring tension on the door is always a little lighter than you think it's going to be.

It opens right up. So welcoming.

"Come on in.

We have something for you.

A place to relieve yourself in exchange for a mental image picture

that will cause you to twitch in your sleep every night for a year and a half . . .

with P.T.S.D."

Portable Toilet Spring Door.

I don't even understand how they're allowed to call this thing a bathroom.

You're crapping in a hole with a box over it.

It's hyena living.

It's beastly.

You want to do that thing your dog does after they go on the grass.

(kicking each rear leg backwards one at a time)

"What are you doing?"

"Just trying to get the last few minutes out of my mind, that's all . . ."

(keeps kicking)

Flex Seal

I would say my favorite show on TV is the Flex Seal infomercial that comes on TV late at night.

If you don't know what Flex Seal is—

It's a miracle.

For people that have leaks and do not want them.

If you have drips, drops, streams, gushing or trickling.

If you're sitting on your roof waiting for a chopper . . . really bad leak.

You get Flex Seal.

Just get it.

Don't "look into it."

We're way past that.

They have a 30-second spot in prime time

and a half-hour infomercial they run late at night which I think is way better.

It's just more leaks.

They go into a lot more depth with each leak.

———

When Flex Seal comes on my TV,

my whole family knows,

"Everybody just shut up.

This is my show.

Just let me watch it.

Look at all these leaks.

This is going to be an unbelievable episode."

I have no idea if any of it is true.

But I need something to believe in.

And I have decided on Flex Seal.

———

I like Phil Swift.

He's the TV spokesman for Flex Seal.

Phil does not seem to think we can hear him.

It's like they said to him,

"Listen, Phil, these people you're talking to, water is pouring into their house.

Everyone's screaming, running around with buckets, sponges and mops.

You've got to project your voice.

And talk fast.

Because once the water rises over their wall outlets and shorts out the TV

that is the end of our sales opportunity.

It's a tight window, so zip it in there."

———

And he does.

He's got a great smile, good energy.

He's got a nice little weight problem going for himself, which is good.

Makes him real.

You believe him.

He looks like a guy that's had a lot of leaks in his life.

A lot of coming home opening his front door

and half of everything he owns just floats by.

Bowling shoes, hot dog buns, MyPillow.

I don't know why but I am 100% sure that Phil Swift has MyPillow.

———

And no, I do not think it is relevant that it's $19.99 for a can of Flex Seal,

to fix a hole in a bucket.

And I know I can get a new bucket for $3.99.

It's not about the bucket.

The point of Flex Seal is just using Flex Seal.

And that's the only problem with Flex Seal.

Because if you do not have a leak, you cannot use it.

Which is the situation I am in,

and where our story takes a heartbreaking turn.

And they don't talk about this in the commercial.

Nobody cares about someone like me,

because they don't know the frustration that you feel

when you have the solution, but you do not have the problem.

I've never had one of my kids come up to me and say,

"Dad, you fixed the leak.

You saved the house.

You're the best."

I've never heard that.

And that's not a hole in a pipe.

That's a hole in your life, and even Flex Seal can't patch that up.

———

And so, I sit there at night

Alone in the dark, the blue TV light just flickering on my face.

Watching the leaks get fixed.

Dreaming my Flex Seal fantasies.

That I somehow, perhaps by mistake,

bought a boat that has a screen door built into the bottom.

Or I bought two halves of a boat that are not joined together.

From a divorce settlement or something.

Who's making boats like this?

How did the salesman get me to overlook these gigantic boat issues?

I don't know the answer to any of these questions, but I know what I'm going to do about it.

And the next scene is me and Phil Swift just zipping through the Everglades.

(Holding outboard tiller.)

Me in my screen-door-bottom boat.

Phil is in his two halves of a boat glued back together.

And we are laughing our fat asses off.

"Hey, Phil!"

"Hey, Jerry!"

That's my dream.

And it's not a wet dream,

thanks to Flex Seal.

Acknowledgments

I would first like to thank George Shapiro, my personal manager and guiding light for so many decades of warm, enthusiastic support and energy. And for sharing thousands of nights with me in our mutual belief that comedy and eating are really all that matters. George and his brilliant partner, Howard West, really built an impressive comedy castle out of my halfway decent twenty-five minutes I came out to LA with in 1980.

I love hanging out with the super-professionals that keep my machine going: Kevin Dochtermann, Rob Prinz, Christian Carino, Tom Keaney, Amy Jacobs, Tammy Johnston, and Yossi Kimberg.

As Georgie always reminds me, "Remember, it's not Show Fun. It's Show Business."

At Simon & Schuster: copy chief Jonathan Evans, designer Paul Dippolito, production director Lisa Erwin, managing editor Kimberly Goldstein, production editor John Paul Jones, assistants Gabby Robles and Maria Mendez, contracts administrator Jeff Wilson, executive editor Sean Manning, art director Jackie Seow, publicity director Julia Prosser, rights director Marie Florio, deputy publisher Richard Rhorer, and my editor and publisher, Jonathan Karp.

I also want to acknowledge Ted Sarandos who, more than anyone else, really changed how the world appreciates stand-up comedy as something maybe a bit more than a way to kill twenty minutes until the music act comes on.

A special thanks to my wonderful sister, Carolyn, who has steadied me so reliably through several hundred varying size crises.

Most important of all is my Wonder of Nature wife, Jessica, who refilled me with life and love at a time when I really was down to empty.

And my kids, Sascha, Julian, and Shepherd, for always looking at me like, "There's something off with this guy . . ."

I have millions of comedy friends and I really do love them all. Especially the way they shake their heads all the time like, "How the hell do you even do this?" And of course, we never really do figure it out. The real point of our lives is that we try anyway.

Index